PUSHING YOUR ENVELOPE

HOW SMART PEOPLE DEFEAT SELF-DOUBT AND LIVE WITH BOLD ENTHUSIASM

MAUREEN ZAPPALA

Copyright © 2018 by Maureen Zappala.

All rights reserved. No part of this publication may be reproduced, distributed or transmitted in any form or by any means, including photocopying, recording, or other electronic or mechanical methods, without the prior written permission of the publisher, except in the case of brief quotations embodied in critical reviews and certain other noncommercial uses permitted by copyright law. For permission requests, write to the publisher, addressed "Attention: Permissions Coordinator," at the address below.

Edited by: Connie Anderson, www.WordsandDeedsInc.com
Cover design: David Leeflang and Gina Zappala

Interior Design: BookDesignTemplates.com

Publisher's Cataloging-in-Publication data

Names: Zappala, Maureen, author.
Title: Pushing your envelope : how smart people defeat self-doubt and live with bold enthusiasm / by Maureen Zappala.
Description: Columbus, OH: Lexington Press, 2018.
Identifiers: ISBN 978-1-881462-57-6
Subjects: LCSH Self-actualization (Psychology.) | Success. | Self-acceptance. | Self-doubt. | BISAC SELF-HELP / Personal Growth / Success
Classification: LCC BF575.S37 .Z37 2018 | DDC 158.1/28--dc23

Lexington Press
2439 Andover Road * Columbus, Ohio 43221

Printed in the United States of America

To every person determined to push their envelope in order to live with bold enthusiasm.

TABLE OF CONTENTS

Acknowledgments   vii
Introduction   ix

PHASE 1: PRESENTING THE PROBLEM

Chapter 1	Houston, We Have a Problem	3
Chapter 2	Over-Achiever, Under-Believer	11
Chapter 3	The Dawn of the Distortion	19
Chapter 4	Own Your Dot	25
Chapter 5	The Symptoms of the Syndrome	35
Chapter 6	Success and Failure	39

PHASE 2: PROCEED WITH A PLAN

Chapter 7	Strategy 1: Examine the Accusation	47
Chapter 8	Strategy 2: Cultivate the Conversation	55
Chapter 9	Strategy 3: Collect Your Documentation	61
Chapter 10	Strategy 4: Build a Strong Foundation	69
Chapter 11	Shifting Your Perspective	79

PHASE 3: PURSUE PEAK PERFORMANCE

Chapter 12	Breaking the Sound Barrier	91
Chapter 13	The Favor in Failure	97
Chapter 14	Fueled Up	101
Chapter 15	Secret Membership in a Secret Club	109

PHASE 4: PERMISSION GRANTED

Chapter 16	Pushing Your Envelope	115

ACKNOWLEDGMENTS

This book not complete without special thanks to everyone who partnered with me, or at least put up with me along the way. I enjoyed the journey because you joined the journey.

Thank you to my "accountability" group of special friends: Michelle Virnelson, Bernice Lopp, Cheryl McConnell, Ann Klunzinger, Julie Sems, and Stephanie Skernivitz. As we met week after week you buoyed me with laughter, encouragement, food and prayer.

Thank you to my wonderful friend and business partner, Jack Park, who constantly celebrated my accomplishments and talents, big and small, allowing me to push forward when I felt empty and discouraged.

Thank you to my peers in the National Speakers Association, who showed me true professionalism, nose-to-the-grindstone commitment, and so many ways to push my envelope. Special thanks to my mastermind group of Lisa Ryan, Lisa Pustelak, Julie Ann Sullivan and Debbie Peterson.

Thank you to the members of the Stage Time University community for your advice, perspective and feedback. Your frequent declaration of "People need this book!" echoed in my head and propelled me forward. It was a privilege to teach the webinar about book publishing. If I had not taught that class at that time, I don't know when this book would be finished. You kept me on my toes.

Thank you to my daughter Gina who not only patiently endured my frequent soliloquies about this topic, and accepted my rabid obsession with completing this book, but offered her brilliant design insights and super-human Photoshop skills to make fabulous tweaks to the book cover and interior layout.

Thank you to God for a bigger vision tied to a grander purpose. And for coffee.

INTRODUCTION

I was almost eight years old when a dream was born. It was about 1969, and I was with my dad in the driveway of our home on Staten Island, New York, hovering over the engine of our family car—a Ford Country Squire "Woodie" station wagon. Dad was doing what he loved the most, which was tinker with cars. I was doing what I loved the most, which was be with Dad.

I liked learning how things worked, and I pummeled my dad with questions. "Daddy, what's that for? What's that do? How does this work?" Finally, he looked at me and said "Maureen, when you grow up, you should be an engineer."

I was appalled. "Ew! No, Daddy!" I groaned, "I don't want to drive a train!"

He laughed and said "No, Maureen, not that kind of engineer! I mean the kind who designs and fixes things, like buildings, bridges and tunnels."

That sparked me. Growing up in New York City, we were surrounded by buildings, bridges and tunnels, which I thought were magnificent. At the time, my dad was part of the design team for the then-under-construction World Trade Center, so the fascination with buildings started at a young age. With newfound delight, I said, "Yes! I will be an engineer."

That's when the dream was born. For my entire education, from grade school through college, I set my sights on becoming an engineer. In 1983, I graduated from the University of Notre Dame with a degree in Mechanical Engineering, and launched a thrilling career as a propulsion researcher with NASA.

Although I never worked on buildings, bridges or tunnels, I found a new love within the aerospace world, working with jet aircraft engines, specifically military fighter engines. Jet propulsion is similar to rocket propulsion, so I can legitimately say I'm a rocket scientist. I admit–that feels pretty cool.

When NASA hired me, I was thrilled, and terrified. Could I do the job? Was I smart enough to work with other super-smart people? Did they realize I was not a straight-A student in college? If only I had paid more attention to some of my engineering classes.

Yet, I pressed on, and spent almost 14 fabulous years at NASA, working on fascinating projects, developing groundbreaking technology. However, I always wondered if I should have done better. I wondered if I made a significant contribution, or held my own against the other engineers in my group. I remember often feeling scared and unqualified, frequently wondering what the heck I was doing. And most of all, I was afraid everyone else would figure out that I didn't belong.

These fears plagued me. I felt pressure to prove myself, and to please my supervisors. I worked hard, and learned mountains of information. However, even when I had gained a level of expertise, and was known around the world in the tight circle of jet propulsion research, I continued to feel like

I was winging it. Would everyone soon figure out that I'm just a scared little girl who's asking the question "How does this work?"

WHY THIS BOOK?

This is the book I wish I'd read back in 1983. I managed to clumsily maneuver my way through fears and self-doubt while at NASA, and on into my second career as a speaker and writer—but it wasn't a conscious or well-constructed journey. I had no master plan or clear-cut agenda. I went from NASA to selling cosmetics, to motherhood, to speaking, to training, and on to writing *and* speaking. With each transition, I felt that familiar pang of self-doubt. Still, I pushed on.

A few years ago, I stumbled on the topic of Impostor Syndrome (IS), the chronic self-doubt that plagues successful and smart people. I thought "Really? There's a name for what I felt?" I had another epiphany moment similar to the one in my Staten Island driveway: "YES! That's what I want to do." A new dream was born: teaching people how to overcome that self-doubt.

As I researched the topic, spoke with scores of people, and reflected on my own experiences, I deconstructed what I did to turn down that volume of self-doubt. I developed strategies to teach others to do the same. Every time I teach these strategies, I am astonished how they resonate with audiences. The resounding chorus was the same: "This is a game changer for me."

These strategies work.

OPERATING ENVELOPES

In the jet-engine industry, the phrase "operating envelope" describes the range of speeds and altitudes that allow safe aircraft engine operation. Every aircraft engine has its own operating envelope. At NASA, we would frequently "push the envelope" to test a new system or piece of hardware. This means we'd run the engine just past its normal safe conditions. Once we established a new safe condition, a new larger operating envelope emerged.

At NASA, I had my own operating envelope. It seemed impressive to others, although it wasn't to me. I imagined it was smaller than it really was. That thinking cost me some opportunities, even though on paper, I accomplished a lot. Living in my little envelope provided me a good dose of fear and concern which robbed me of the chance to enjoy the success I actually had. I stayed small, and sometimes even invisible. Since then, I've learned to push my envelope, and turn down the volume of that limiting "impostor fear." I discovered how to live with more bold enthusiasm, embrace my success and own my accomplishments. In this book, you'll find simple and effective strategies that can help you do the same thing. You can be freed from the grip of the impostor fears, so you can push the envelope of your self-imposed limitations. You can be bolder and more courageous. You can take more risks, and truly enjoy your success.

It's simple but not easy. Of course, nothing of great worth in life is easy. It's scary, frustrating and costly, but to stay small and invisible is worse because it births regrets that will burden you. It will cause anxiety that will paralyze you. And it will rob the world of the brilliance you have to offer. It's time to push your envelope. The world needs your greatness.

PHASE 1

PRESENTING THE PROBLEM

CHAPTER 1

HOUSTON, WE HAVE A PROBLEM

It was late 1983. I was brand-new mechanical engineer, fresh out of college, at my new job at NASA's Lewis Research Center in Cleveland. I was a Project Engineer in the Propulsion Systems Laboratory, a jet-engine test facility. We called it "PSL" for short.

This was my dream job. As an aviation fan, I knew that PSL was a landmark on the landscape of aircraft engine research. Every aircraft flying today uses technology developed in PSL. I was completely geeked out to be there.

My first assignment at PSL was simple: observe an engine test. How hard was that? I just had to show up, and shut up.

That first day, I stepped into the control room and was instantly awed. It was surreal. The walls were filled with TV screens, lights, knobs, and dials. The countertops were strewn with keyboards and clipboards. People on headsets were murmuring to each other. I thought, "Oh my gosh! It looks just like Mission Control! This is beautiful!" I was in Techie Utopia.

About a dozen engineers and technicians filled the room. The mood was intense. The lead test engineer was a mountain of a man, like Mount Everest, only bigger, with glasses. He had a steely, stern look, and clearly was the boss. Everything happened under his watch. Nothing happened without his okay. He scared me.

Regardless, I had a job to do. Scanning the room, I spotted an open chair against the back wall. I thought, "That seat's mine!" I slinked into the room and slithered along the wall. I reached the chair, plopped my little bottom down, and began to do my job.

I watched. And I watched. And I watched.

The test progressed well, and I began to relax.

I didn't know exactly what was happening, but suddenly I sensed we were on the crucial edge of a technical breakthrough. You could feel it. The room felt tense. Everyone hushed. We leaned in.

Then we all heard it.

"Hiccup!"

Oh my gosh. Seriously?

"Hiccup!"

It was me. In the midst of breathless silence, on the cusp of a stupendous discovery, I got the hiccups.

Did you ever feel every bit of dignity slide out of your body?

A dozen heads snapped in my direction. I wanted to disappear.

Did I mention that I was the only woman?

I could almost read their minds. "Who's *she*? Who let *her* in? What's *she* doing here?" My heart raced, and I felt stupid.

I locked eyes with Mount Everest. I thought, "I wonder if he heard me?" Of course he heard me; the far reaches of the universe heard me. I thought, "This is it! My career is over before it started!" Time stood still. I was nervous. The crew was nervous. I think even God was nervous.

Maybe you're thinking "Maureen, come on! Everyone gets the hiccups. What's the big deal?"

I agree. Hiccups happen. However, this story is a metaphor for something that affects capable and accomplished people. Many of them live in fear that they're just a hiccup away from others discovering that they are just plain stupid. They feel incompetent and unqualified. It's as if they're masquerading and trying to fit in, but in fact they feel like a fake. It's called Impostor Syndrome, and is a chronic self-doubt that plagues successful, smart, and influential people. It's an inability or unwillingness to look objectively at the data that describes their success, and prevents them from embracing the fact that they are indeed successful, smart and influential. It taunts and haunts them with accusations that demean their accomplishments, creates doubts about their capabilities, and forces them to remain small and hidden.

Does that describe you? It fit me.

Thankfully, Mount Everest didn't toss me from the control room that day. He simply smiled and went on with his work. Everyone did. My blunder was big only to me because my thinking was distorted. That's good news because thought distortions, including impostor fears, can be corrected with thought adjustments.

I made a good decision to stay working in that control room. Nine years later, I was promoted to the manager of PSL. We did exciting and cutting-edge work in PSL that made my journey into a joy ride. However, as I mentioned in the introduction, that fraud-fear never completely left me. It haunted me for years, keeping me quiet, small and invisible, in spite of my track record of success. It's paradoxical that while I had a position of influence and responsibility, I was afraid to speak up, stand up, and stand out.

That's a problem.

"WE'RE NOT TAKING THAT ON!"

In PSL, when we received a test request from a customer, we immediately met with them to discuss the problem they were trying to solve. In many cases, this initial problem led to other problems which led to other solutions, which led to other test programs, which led to other groups getting involved, which led to more resources, more money, more time, more data and more studies. It got complicated, but the payoff was almost always worth it. Tackling a tough problem at the beginning created a vehicle for being able to solve a bundle of other technical challenges down the road.

I recall one such situation at NASA. In the mid 1980s, I was sitting in a meeting with Frank, my boss's boss, the strong, smart, and intense chief of our division. He sat motionless at the head of the conference table. His tight jaw and furrowed brow emphasized his authority. I was nervous and silent as I waited for his decision. I had just presented a formal proposal for a new engine test at the request of one of our sister centers, NASA-Dryden and we needed Frank's approval to proceed. The test was an exciting one. Dryden was preparing to conduct flight tests on a completely different type of supersonic aircraft, the X-29 Forward Swept Wing, and they needed specific data on a General Electric F-404 turbofan engine to use during the flight tests. PSL was perfectly equipped to gather the data. I laid out their proposal, and included my recommendations for the test hardware, how we'd structure the test to meet the test objectives, and why the test would be significant to us. I was so hoping he would approve it.

His silence seemed eternal. Suddenly, he spoke. "There's no way we're taking that on. We're not agreeing to do that test."

Excuse me? What did he just say? I was shocked.

I was intimidated too. He seemed grumpy as he snapped, "Look Maureen, the facility schedule is already too tight. Manpower is limited. Funding isn't adequate. We can't meet the deadline. And this test has no value to the agency. There's no valid reason to do the test."

I couldn't argue with his points. At that moment, I felt powerless, and I hated that feeling.

Deeply discouraged, I shuffled back to my office and called the Dryden folks with the bad news. They needed this data, so they didn't want to give up. I truly thought the test was too cool to let go. This aircraft was so unique and unusual, and I *really* wanted PSL to be part of this adventure. I invited Dryden to beef up the proposal, and then visit us to present the improved version. I invited other NASA groups to join the meeting, hoping to get them to jump on board with the program. That would provide extra funding and additional visibility which would give us an advantage in prioritizing it in the schedule.

This worked beautifully. During the meeting, we all discovered more reasons to conduct the test program, so we were able to piggyback other tests on top of the flight data program. What started out as a simple calibration test had evolved into a wide-reaching technology-development program.

And yes, it was beyond cool to be part of it.

What does this have to do with the Impostor Syndrome? Most people don't know what this condition is. Most people who struggle with it don't have a name for it, but they're well acquainted with the feeling that something is oddly amiss. Maybe they're an entrepreneur, an artist or a professional. They probably have a good position in a great company, with a decent paycheck. Maybe they're in management or a position of influence. Yet, this weird self-doubt plagues them. Some people may call it a lack of confidence or low self-esteem, but it's only loosely tied to those. This self-doubt plagues their inner thoughts, and accuses them of feeling like a fake on the job.

When I speak about this topic, I always ask, "Have you ever heard of the Impostor Syndrome?" Maybe a third to half my audience nods. Then, as I describe it, I see their eyes light up and their heads lift up. They see hope for a problem that they didn't even know was real.

The Impostor Syndrome is complicated. There are a lot of facets to it, from its origin to its symptoms, to its impact on your performance in your job. If you chose to unravel it, it's not going to be easy. It's going to shove a lot of things off the radar of your world. It's going to need to be prioritized ahead of strategies that have been working up till now. It's going to cost you effort, time, and focus. And maybe like Frank, in his hesitation to take on the F404 test, you don't think there's a legitimate reason to take on this effort.

But there is. If you tackle the problem, if you put the full force of your will to overcome this struggle, if you choose to realign your resources and thinking and energy, you'll solve a boatload of other problems in your world. Unlike what Frank said, there *is* a legitimate reason to take this on.

If you face these impostor fears, you can:

- Embrace the reality of your intelligence, your capability, your potential, and your influence.
- Be comfortable with taking risks when you realize they cannot ultimately destroy you.
- State with appropriate pride, "I am a creative, intelligent and influential person that has so much to offer."
- Silence the voice that speaks to you on the edge of a great achievement, sneering, "Who do you think you are?"
- Find like-minded people who can partner with you on the journey so it's not as intimidating.
- Be comfortable being competitive.
- Objectively state your competencies without shame, apology or dismissal.
- Learn to let go of exhausting perfectionism without compromising your commitment to quality.
- Be free to invest yourself into other's lives without feeling obligated, pressured or manipulated.
- Dream and make that dream happen.
- Define success by your own terms.
- Live with bold enthusiasm.

Dare to take on the problem of your Impostor Syndrome. Dare to find the courage and resources to push your envelope. Don't be like Frank. Be free.

CHAPTER 2

OVER-ACHIEVER, UNDER-BELIEVER

The Impostor Syndrome, also called Impostor Phenomenon, is an inability to own your success. It's as if you look at the objective data, the facts that say, "You are successful," but you don't see it. When you see all this great information on paper, the accolades, the achievements, the accomplishments, it's as if you're looking at someone else's resume, not your own. You don't make the connection between you and the information about you. Or, if you're pushed to acknowledge them, you minimize the successes by explaining them away as a mistake, luck, being in the right place at the right time, or having the right people put in a good word for you.

It's not the same as humility or false modesty. Humility is graciously accepting the truth of the facts about your success without being boastful or prideful. False modesty is *internally* accepting the facts, but *outwardly* pretending to not accept them. Neither humility nor false modestly reflect the Impostor Syndrome, because Impostor Syndrome is a cognitive distortion of the facts, or a distorted thought process. For example these are typical beliefs and conclusions:

- You genuinely think you're not as good or smart as people think you are.
- You are puzzled at how you came into your success, and almost expect it to evaporate in a flash.
- You don't intend to be a phony, but you feel like it. You live in fear of being uncovered as the incompetent that you know you are.
- You feel like you've pulled the wool over everyone's eyes.
- You don't intend to be deceptive, but now the fear of being uncovered propels you to continue the "ruse."

Yet, there's a part of you that acknowledges that you can at least do a decent job, so you continue to do what you are doing, all the while feeling like you're faking it.

Can you see how complicated this gets?

Before we move on, I want introduce a new term. The bulky, chunky and clunky phrase "those who suffer from Impostor Syndrome" is a mouthful to say, and lots to type. Something simpler is needed.

Since this person (let's just say it's a man) who suffers from the Impostor Syndrome is indeed smart, successful and accomplished, he may likely be described as an "over-achiever." But he discounts his own success and disbelieves his own great press. That makes him an "under-believer." I now will refer to him (and others like him) as an "over-achiever, under-believer" and use the abbreviation OAUB. Phew. That takes a lot of pressure off me, when talking and writing/typing. In the next few chapters, you'll learn the symptoms that characterize OAUB, and some practical strategies that will help turn self-doubt into self-belief.

TAKE THE IMPOSTOR TEST

Most people admit to feeling self-doubt at some point in their life. Most people have experienced a level of fear or uncertainty when faced with a new challenge. Does this mean they're all feeling like an impostor? No. Isolated self-doubt or occasional trepidation is part of being human, but there are other symptoms that, taken as a collective whole, do point toward this impostor experience. This quiz below[1] can help determine if, and how strongly, you cross swords with this foe of fraudulence.

For each question, circle the number that best indicates how true the statement is as it relates to you. It is best to give the first response that enters your mind rather than dwelling on each statement and thinking about it over and over.

1. I have often succeeded on a test or task even though I was afraid that I would not do well before I undertook the task.
   1   2   3   4   ⑤
   (never true) (rarely) (sometimes) (often) (always true)

2. I can give the impression that I'm more competent than I really am.
   1   2   3   4   ⑤

3. I avoid evaluations if possible and have a dread of others evaluating me.

---

[1] (Note: This Clance IP test is from the book "The Impostor Phenomenon: When Success Makes You Feel Like A Fake" (pp. 20-22), by P.R. Clance, 1985, Toronto: Bantam Books. Copyright 1985 by Pauline Rose Clance, Ph.D., ABPP. Reprinted by permission. Do not reproduce without permission from Pauline Rose Clance, drpaulinerose@comcast.net, www.paulineroseclance.com.)

1   2   3   4   (5)

4. When people praise me for something I've accomplished, I'm afraid I won't be able to live up to their expectations of me in the future.
   1   2   3   4   (5)

5. I sometimes think I obtained my present position or gained my present success because I happened to be in the right place at the right time or knew the right people.
   1   2   (3)   4   5

6. I'm afraid people important to me may find out that I'm not as capable as they think I am.
   1   2   (3)   4   5

7. I tend to remember the incidents in which I have not done my best more than those times I have done my best.
   1   2   3   (4)   5

8. I rarely do a project or task as well as I'd like to do it.
   1   2   3   (4)   5

9. Sometimes I feel or believe that my success in my life or in my job has been the result of some kind of error.
   1   2   (3)   4   5

10. It's hard for me to accept compliments or praise about my intelligence or accomplishments.
    1   2   3   4   (5)

11. At times, I feel my success has been due to some kind of luck.
    1   2   (3)   4   5

12. I'm disappointed at times in my present accomplishments and think I should have accomplished much more.

1   2   3   4   ⑤

13. Sometimes I'm afraid others will discover how much knowledge or ability I really lack.
    1   2   ③   4   5

14. I'm often afraid that I may fail at a new assignment or undertaking even though I generally do well at what I attempt.
    1   2   3   4   ⑤

15. When I've succeeded at something and received recognition for my accomplishments, I have doubts that I can keep repeating that success.
    1   2   3   ④   5

16. If I receive a great deal of praise and recognition for something I've accomplished, I tend to discount the importance of what I've done.
    1   2   3   ④   5

17. I often compare my ability to those around me and think they may be more intelligent than I am.
    1   2   ③   4   5

18. I often worry about not succeeding with a project or examination, even though others around me have considerable confidence that I will do well.
    1   2   3   ④   5

19. If I'm going to receive a promotion or gain recognition of some kind, I hesitate to tell others until it is an accomplished fact.
    1   2   3   ④   5

20. I feel bad and discouraged if I'm not "the best" or at least "very special" in situations that involve achievement.
    1   2   3   4   ⑤

$$5 - 8 \times 5 = 40$$
$$4 - 6 \times 4 = 24$$
$$3 - 6 \times 3 = \underline{18}$$
$$82$$

After taking the Impostor Test, add together the numbers of the responses to each statement. If the total score is 40 or less, you have few Impostor characteristics; if the score is between 41 and 60, you have moderate impostor experiences; a score between 61 and 80 means you frequently have Impostor feelings; and a score higher than 80 means you often have intense impostor experiences. The higher the score, the more frequently and seriously the Impostor Syndrome/Phenomenon will interfere in your life.

If your score is higher than you thought it would be, relax. It doesn't mean you have a disease or a destructive psychological condition. In fact, many successful people who live with Impostor Syndrome lead perfectly normal lives. It's only when the condition starts to interfere with their life does it become a problem.

It can interfere when the pressure of perfection gets too much, or the disappointment of not achieving goals is too great, or the fear of new challenges paralyzes you. It can be a real problem which leads to other issues like depression, anxiety, and high blood pressure.

Maybe you're just tired of feeling like a fake. You're exhausted from trying to make sure that the thin veneer of your capability is not scratched by a casual question or a failure, causing the whole world to mock you, scorn you, and toss you to the curb. (Although, as you'll read in this book, that probably won't ever happen.)

Whatever your Impostor Syndrome experience is, you can learn to prosper and flourish in spite of it. You can live with bold enthusiasm, free from the gripping fear of being found out as a fraud. You may not completely eliminate it, nor should you. A healthy dose of self-doubt can be good. It forces you to check your motives and evaluate your circumstances. It allows humility to step in to keep your ego in check. If you've ever seen an episode of the audition portion of the TV show, "The Voice," you've seen people who could use a dose of this healthy self-doubt. They are the ones who, in contrast to Impostor Syndrome sufferers, have no clue that they truly lack talent, and think they are way more talented and significant than they are. That also has a name: Dunning Kruger effect, which describes people who are poor performers but are completely (and often arrogantly) unaware of their own deficiencies. Somewhere on the continuum between over-estimating and underestimating your skill, ability and worth, is a healthy and peaceful acceptance where you can thrive.

Aim not to eliminate the impostor voice, but rather to turn down the volume. That's huge. When you do, you'll stop shrinking back in your field, you'll take a bolder position in your workplace, you'll feel ready to reach up and reach out for growth opportunities. When you learn to turn down the impostor's volume, everything gets better. ☺

CHAPTER 3

THE DAWN OF THE DISTORTION

Let's go back to the beginning. The Impostor Syndrome (also called Impostor Phenomenon) was first described in 1978 by Drs. Pauline Clance and Suzanne Imes, two clinical psychologists from Atlanta, Georgia. In their practice, they worked with a lot of highly intelligent professional women and brilliant female grad students who came for therapy to overcome things like conflict, depression, and anxiety. Some were overwhelmed with new and greater responsibilities, or were facing creative challenges in their jobs or research—and the stress was spilling into other areas of their lives. As Drs. Clance and Imes worked them through these frontline issues, they heard consistent sideline issues, which included a repeated chorus of "I don't deserve my success," and "I'm afraid of being found out as a fraud." Most of these women consistently struggled with self-doubt and were frustrated about not progressing in their fields. Fascinated, the therapists researched further, interviewing 150 high-achieving women on the topic of self-doubt. They documented their findings in a paper called, "The Impostor Phenomenon in High-

Achieving Women: Dynamics and Therapeutic Interventions." Drs. Clance and Imes had no idea how much impact their research would have.

This topic has gained steady ground since then, showing up in an avalanche of research papers and psychology journal articles. Valerie Young's 2011 fascinating book, *The Secret Thoughts of Successful Women: Why Capable People Suffer from the Impostor Syndrome and How to Thrive in Spite of it*, brought the topic to our culture's center stage. In 2013, Sheryl Sandburg, the CEO of Facebook, released her book, *Lean In*, in which she admitted to her own struggles with impostor-ism. That same year, another influential businesswoman, Joyce Rochè, the retired former CEO of Girls Inc (the behemoth nonprofit that was formerly Girls Clubs of America), as well as a former executive VP at Avon, released her impostor-confessing book, *The Empress Has No Clothes: Conquering Self-Doubt to Embrace Success*. In addition, the research has gone from widespread surveys and anecdotal reports to significant neuroscience studies connecting the brain and emotions. It's exciting to see what's developing on this topic.

The Impostor Phenomenon was originally thought to be something that only affected women. Drs. Clance and Imes targeted women specifically because they saw the pattern there first. In 1993, Dr. Clance confirmed that men are just as likely as women to doubt their ability, discount their success, and feel undeserving of the praise they receive. In 2012, psychologist and Ivy League associate professor Amy Cuddy delivered a TED talk about body language, where she described how she felt like she didn't belong in the world of post-secondary education, and how she felt like a fake. After the talk, she received thousands of emails from people saying they felt it too. Half of those emails were from men. So, while it resonates with women, it's a condition that also hits men, although not with the same intensity, and not with the same impact. Men and women processes it differently.

It's estimated that up to 70 percent of high-performing people have experienced impostor feelings. For some people, it's debilitating and paralyzing. Ironically, it's most prevalent in highly successful people, the ones who strive for excellence, achievement, and accomplishment. Margie Warrell, author of the books, *Stop Playing Safe,* and *Find Your Courage,* writes, "The Impostor Syndrome is the domain of the high achiever; those who set the bar low are rarely its victim."

It's not necessarily a bad thing. Warrell adds encouragement by pointing out that people who self identify as OAUBs usually seek excellence over mediocrity, aim for great goals and do what it takes to reach them. These are admirable qualities, for sure. The low achievers don't hear the voice of the impostor. High achievers do. Managers, leaders, technical experts, and people with a lot of history and experience hear it. The trick is to not let it paralyze you or hold you back. In fact, if you are identifying yourself as an impostor, there's great hope. You can be released. The first step is recognizing the grip the impostor has, so you can take the steps to be released. You've won the first battle. As Dr. Phil McGraw says, "You can't change what you don't acknowledge." So, kudos to you for acknowledging it. Let's move on to getting past it.

WHO DOES IT AFFECT?

Impostor Syndrome typically affects people in careers where the daily work is not scripted, choreographed or predictable. Each day is a new challenge or new set of circumstances. It's most common in the science, technology, engineering and mathematics (STEM) fields like computer programming, information systems, manufacturing, product design, research & development (R&D), and medicine. The tremendous proliferation of information in the sciences contributes to the feeling of impostor-ism. Considering the lightening speed at which technology develops, it's no wonder that technical experts feel overwhelmed trying to keep up with it. Not only do they feel the pressure to master what they have already learned, but there's also so much more coming at them that they need to learn quickly. There's pressure to keep up with journals, reports, developments, new products, new approaches, and new data. It's dizzying. When a professional peer seems to solve problems quickly, it's easy to feel stupid in comparison. I'm sure you've often said "Why didn't *I* think of that?" or "How did I not see that solution?" Instead, you look at your failures and shortfalls while all around you it seems that others are finding success so much easier and solutions so much faster.

The art, design, and creative world is another petri dish of impostor-ism. Creative people must constantly come up with a new design, a new pitch, a new piece of art, or a new ad campaign. Add in the pressure of a deadline or demanding client, and the fraud fears are intensified. Putting your artistic self on the line is so risky because rejection is very possible. If you're a creative person in the tech industry, in a job such as a web designer or a gaming designer, you get a double dose of insecurity.

It affects people in academia, especially at the graduate level. Grad students, professors, and teaching assistants all experience self-doubt as they compare themselves to their peers who appear to be much smarter. There's pressure to produce stellar research results, compete for limited grant money, and work to achieve tenure. Getting published, striving for prestige, comparing yourself to international experts—it's overwhelming. Imagine being a professor at Massachusetts Institute of Technology (MIT), which claims about 80 Nobel Laureates in its history. How can one measure up to that?

Entrepreneurs, CEOs, and people who've made career changes also feel the sting of this experience. It's common in fields where people are highly educated and credentialed, like law, finance, management and politics. Entertainers, sales professionals, social workers, marketing specialists, and newspaper columnists are all affected. Celebrities like Sally Field, Maya Angelou, and Tina Fay have confessed it. I already mentioned that Sheryl Sandberg, COO of Facebook, claims it. So have Starbucks CEO Howard Schultz, performers Natalie Portman, Tom Hanks, and even Lady Gaga. The list includes tennis pro Serena Williams; Editor-in-chief of ELLE magazine, Justine Cullen; author John Steinbeck; and the influential John Lee Dumas, creator of the hugely successful podcast EOFire. Even me, a former NASA propulsion engineer.

The common thread is that these people are in fields that are creative, innovative, and even competitive. They also often lack significant mentoring. The "Lone-Ranger" mentality is prevalent, but it may be because intelligent people are less likely to seek out the mentors in the first place. Or it could be that a corporate culture or professional environment doesn't understand or fully embrace the value of mentoring.

Other causes that lead someone to feel like an OAUB are found in the family of origin, the specific professional path, race and gender identity, and even the specific corporate culture. Some companies inadvertently foster a more intense impostor culture with their structure for reward and recognition, promotion or competitiveness. Even the ubiquitous "Employee of the Month" recognition can incite unhealthy competition, cause the more "Steady-Eddie" performers to lose interest and become disengaged, and foster resentment toward the employees who consistently win.

This is clearly a widespread issue. It not only affects individuals, but entire organizations. If an OAUB is in the ranks, his chronic self-doubt could hold him back from reaching for an opportunity like a promotion or special assignment. If management is unaware that the talent is right there in their own employee pool, they'd fill the role with a less-qualified person, or spend extra resources to fill the job with an outside new hire. It's a shame. Everyone loses when an OAUB shrinks back in self-doubt.

Chapter 4

OWN YOUR DOT

When I speak on this topic of Impostor Syndrome, I'm always amazed at how people respond. I've spoken for corporations, associations, volunteer organizations, community groups, entrepreneur groups, and churches. This topic resonates with the smartest of the smart. And even though I've developed extremely effective *strategies* that help the OAUB, this one particular *concept* seems to rise above the rest. It's the one idea that people remember the most, which tells me it's the one they need the most. I call it "Own Your Dot," and it is a great visual representation of the cognitive distortion of the Impostor Syndrome.

Let's represent your expertise with a dot, as shown in the figure on the next page. Let's call this dot which represents all you know in your specific field, "The stuff I know." It's a great dot. You've worked hard to fill your dot with your expertise. You probably like the dot. You chose the field to enter, and you felt comfortable in it, so filling your dot was enjoyable and often easy. Sometimes maybe it was hard to fill the dot, and other times, the dot wasn't so much fun, but it's still your dot. You earned it.

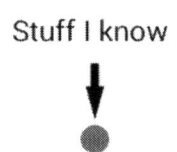

Stuff I know
↓
●

When you're by yourself, your dot seems pretty special, but when you get around other people in your field, something happens. Suddenly you fear that your dot isn't what others think it should be. You think that others expect your dot to be bigger, more impressive.

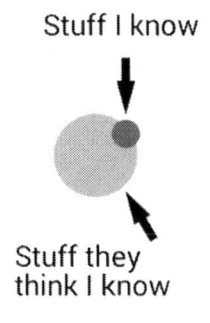

Stuff I know
↓
●
↑
Stuff they
think I know

You call this bigger dot "Stuff they think I know." You feel a bit embarrassed that your real dot doesn't measure up to their imagined dot. Then you feel shame because you think your dot *should* be as big and impressive as that fake dot you *think* they see, so you start to act as if that fake dot really is your dot.

But it gets worse. As you look at one of your peers, you imagine her dot is even bigger than your fake big dot. It not only includes your real dot and your fake dot, but a whole lot of other "stuff" that you didn't even know existed. This is the "stuff that I think everyone else knows." And of course, you imagine the size of that dot approaches infinity, which is the mathematical term for "no limit." Simply put, you think, "She knows so much more than I do! She's way more sophisticated and prepared and knowledgeable and competent than I am."

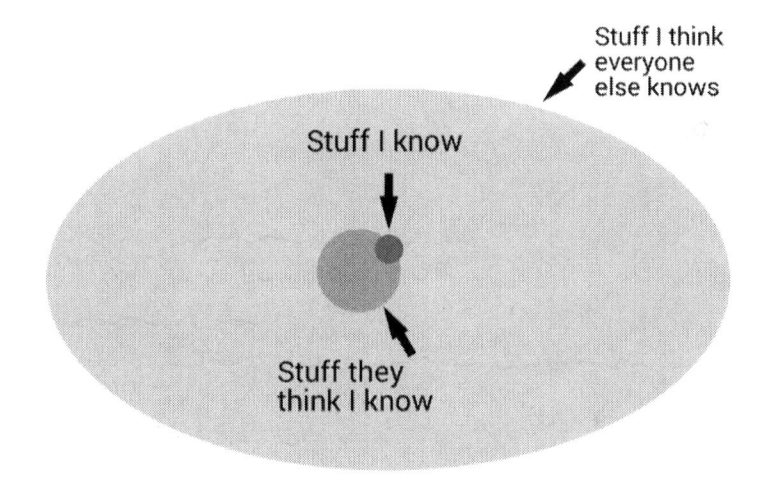

Stuff I think everyone else knows

Stuff I know

Stuff they think I know

But it's a distortion of your thought process. The reality is quite different, and much more optimistic.

Here's the reality. Yes, you have your own dot. It's your stuff that you know. You earned it, and it's all yours. Your peers have dots too. They all do. Their dots are similar to yours, but they're different. Let's call their dots "The stuff that everyone else knows," and represent it with dots that are the same size, but different shades.

```
        Stuff I know
             ↓
    Stuff
    everyone
    else knows
```

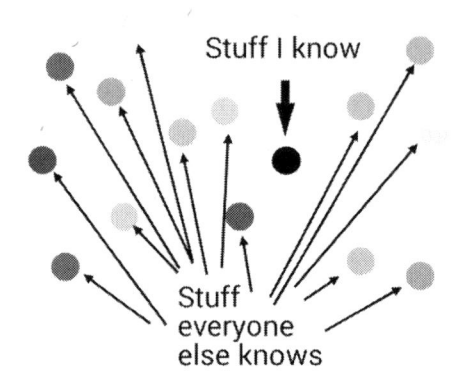

Just like you, they worked hard to fill their dot with what they currently know. They probably like and feel comfortable with their dot. Sometimes filling their dot was easy and enjoyable. Sometimes it wasn't, but it's their dot, and it's not the same as yours. We all have different dots. Some dots overlap and some dots have different content or application, or came from different perspectives. No two dots are the same. One is no better or worse, more or less useful, more or less valuable than any other dot. There is no reason to think your dot is any less significant than their dot.

This is truth. You know a lot of stuff. Brilliant stuff. Stuff you've accumulated, learned, and internalized. It came from your education, your observations, your family background, your life experiences, who you know, what you've read, where you've visited. All this tremendously valuable information is housed in your dot. It's a great dot. It's an awesome dot. And it's totally your dot. The person next to you...guess what? They have a great dot, too. It's their dot, filled with their great stuff, brilliant stuff that they've accumulated, learned and internalized.

It gets even better.

Let's overlap all the dots with a gigantic dot that represents all knowledge, known and unknown. Let's call it "All stuff that can possibly be known." Its size approaches infinity. Even if you put everyone's dots together, including all knowledge from every person across time and space, the sum total will not equal the sum total of all information that can possibly be known. Knowledge is ever increasing, and there is so much that has yet to be discovered.

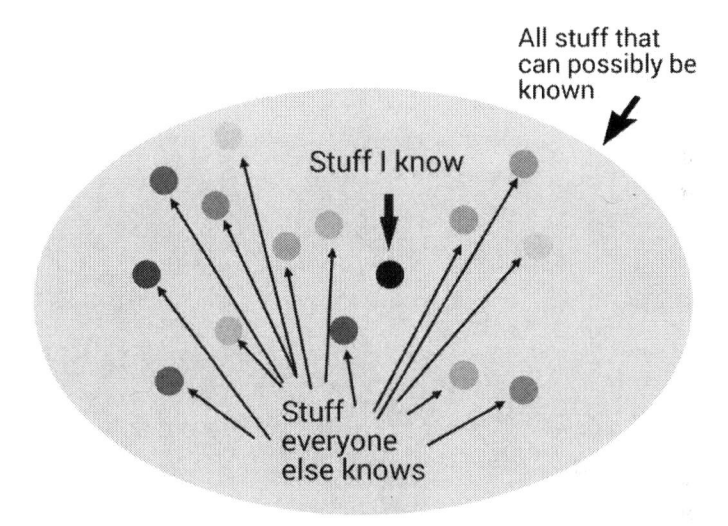

Not a single person or a single group of people on earth can possibly know all that stuff. Why do you think that you are substandard because you know different stuff than someone else? Understanding this perspective is essential for you to grasp your own greatness. You greatness cannot be diminished because of dot-envy.

EINSTEIN

Perhaps you're thinking, "No Maureen, my dot is not the same as everyone else's! I'm no Einstein! I'm not *that* smart."

Your dot is not a measure of intelligence alone. In fact, Einstein himself doubted his own accomplishments. He was plagued with self-doubt that was born from his sluggish academic growth in grade school, when experts assumed he was mentally challenged. He was slow to learn, slow to speak, and failed his first college entrance exam. He loved science and pursued it with rabid fascination. He's quoted as saying, "Don't worry about your difficulties in mathematics. I assure you mine are much greater."

When he revealed his Theory of Relativity, he upended the science world. However, he almost blew it. He was just days away from being beaten to the finish line by another scientist. According to a March 2018 *Quantum Magazine* article, after spending years developing his theory, Einstein was close to finalizing it, but discovered a critical error in his assumptions that he had made two years earlier. He panicked. He knew that a fellow scientist, German mathematician David Hilbert, was close to revealing his own theory of relativity. Einstein jumped into action, corrected his erroneous assumption and for days, furiously reworked his entire theory. It was a race between these two men. Einstein won. In November 1918 he unveiled his theory in a series of lectures to the Prussian Academy of Science. A landmark in history was made by a man who had a tough time in math.

If Einstein, who accepted his own shortcomings, was able to push forward and own his dot, so can you.

SWITCHING DOTS

Are you still not convinced that your dot is special? Let's put things in context, and make it truly objective with a powerful exercise. We'll take you out of the equation for a moment.

Consider this list of people, well known for a certain talent or field of expertise:

Michael Jordan	basketball
Barbara Streisand	singing
Pablo Picasso	abstract art
Martha Stewart	cooking and decorating
Mr. Rogers	children's entertainment
Katie Couric	TV news personality
Jerry Seinfeld:	comedian
Babe Ruth	baseball
Neil Armstrong	astronaut
Warren Buffet	businessman
Jeff Gordon	NASCAR racer
Mikhail Baryshnikov	dancer
Billy Graham	evangelist

These people are great at what they do. Their dots are well known, and in fact define them in many ways. When you say "Michael Jordan" most people automatically think basketball.

Here's the exercise: Pick two people from the list above, for example, Pablo Picasso and Neil Armstrong. Pretend they tried to switch dots. Can you imagine Pablo Picasso doing what it took to walk on the moon? Or Armstrong painting these abstract cubist images that took the art world by storm? It's ludicrous on many levels. For one thing, Picasso didn't live in the era of technology that Armstrong did. Armstrong may have been artistic (I don't know) but clearly his commitment to aerospace engineering, the U.S. space program, and his astronaut training, eclipsed any artistic tendencies. They couldn't possibly switch dots.

What if Jerry Seinfeld switched dots with Martha Stewart? Or Mikhail Baryshnikov switched with Billy Graham? It seems absurd to imagine the outstanding skills of one expert belonging to another. It seems silly to even imagine them trying to do what the other person does well. Barbara Streisand hitting home runs like Babe Ruth? Warren Buffet keeping company with Mr. Roger's puppets? I don't think so. More importantly, we don't discount a single person on that list because they don't have the skills of another person. Katie Couric is no less impressive because she doesn't race a car like Jeff Gordon.

If it's hard to imagine people switching dots, why do you do it to yourself? ? ? ?

- Do you have "dot envy"?
- Why do you wish you had someone else's dot?
- Why do you discount yourself because you don't have someone else's dot?
- Why don't you value your own dot? Your dot is special. You are special.

I'm starting to sound like Barney the Dinosaur. By the way, he's got a great dot, too. He managed to keep my kids mesmerized when they were little.

Okay, maybe you're thinking, "Maureen, your analogy doesn't make sense because you're comparing experts across different industries. What about people in *my* industry? I feel stupid next to them."

Fine, let's look at experts in a given field, say, the music entertainment industry. Can you picture a crooner like Tony Bennett singing a head-banging rock song like David Lee Roth? Or Dolly Parton ripping out a rap song like Eminem? Or the Beatles doing disco like the BeeGees? Probably not. And that's okay. They own their dot, and are no less impressive because their dots are different.

I don't want to beat this topic to a pulp, but it's important to understand it. In your circle of influence, you have expertise, experience, and opinions that others don't have. You are probably even considered *an expert at something*. Be proud of that (in the appropriate way, not the haughty, obnoxious way.) You don't need to be *the expert*. Being an expert is just as significant and worthy.

If you don't think you are an expert, stick around. You'll see later in this book how you can adjust your thinking and be free and comfortable to admit, "Yes, I'm good at that. I did well at that. I deserve that promotion or award." It is only in that freedom will you flourish as an OAUB.

CHAPTER 5

THE SYMPTOMS OF THE SYNDROME

Contrary to what people think, the Impostor Syndrome is not a lack of confidence, but rather a cluster of symptoms that together accuse you of feeling like a fraud. When you learn the symptoms, it's easier to defeat the self-doubt. You cannot overcome an enemy if you cannot recognize enemy. If you are an OAUB, here are the most common symptoms:

1. The Impostor Cycle

If you are faced with a new assignment, chances are you typically respond in one of two ways: you either over-prepare (work like crazy to eliminate any possibility of failure) or procrastinate (delay until the last possible moment because you're not exactly sure what to do, and then work like crazy.) The result is usually the same: you do a phenomenal job. The outcome is outstanding. Everyone is thrilled and impressed with you. There's hefty praise and applause. While people are still cheering, you breathe a huge sigh of relief.

However, you're not relieved because you think you did a good job, but because you think, "Whew! That was close! They almost figured out I didn't know what I was doing!" Then panic grips you because you think, "Oh my gosh...I need to do it again for the next project." The cycle repeats, and you never enjoy your own success.

2. The Need to be Special or the Best

You want to feel special, perhaps unique or privileged, and definitely different from everyone else. Maybe it's your background, or personal experience that is special. Maybe it's a connection to a celebrity or influential person that makes you feel it. Whatever it is, you will seek to find some way to set yourself apart. You may also be a perfectionist, one who sees your value tied to your performance. You feel judged by an unmerciful and inescapable report card that measures your every movement against some ultimate (yet evasive) standard of perfection. Everything must be flawless. You say to yourself, "If I *do* good, I *am* good. If I hang around special people, I am a special person."

3. Superman/Superwoman Complex

Related to the perfectionist, the superman/woman is one who doesn't delegate well. You think it's all on your shoulders, and nobody else can do it well. You may think asking for help is a sign of weakness, or something that puts a burden on someone else. You feel the pressure to do it all, and do it all perfectly. The dirty little secret is: while you are spinning all these plates and keeping the earth on its axis, your real (often unconscious) motive is to look as busy as possible so as to give the appearance of being effective. Ironically, you *are* effective, and don't realize that asking for help can make you look even more effective. Humility is actually extremely attractive, but you don't believe that.

4. Use of Charm/Insight/Humor

[margin note: OA over achiever / UB under believer]

OAUBs are utterly charming and magnetic, especially toward people in authority or influence. They look up to superiors, and do what they can to impress them or win their approval. They'll add insightful comments to conversations to appear relevant, even if they're not entirely familiar with the topic of the conversation. They may know just enough to sound smart. Their strategy is this: "If I can throw in a fact or comment that's somewhat related to the topic, that's better because in my mind, being silent equals being stupid." They can be very witty and entertaining, because they think, "If I can keep them laughing, they won't notice I'm stupid."

5. Fear of Failure

We all fear failure, and we all will try to hide or misdirect attention from a flaw or mistake. So, there's a little bit of phoniness in all of us. This "fear of failure" symptom is different. When it gets so intense that it causes you to consistently aim lower than you're capable of, everyone loses. When it becomes a shield of inauthenticity that hides your best, and calls you to a hyper-vigilant practice of personal image management (i.e., protecting your dignity at all costs), that's exhausting.

6. Fear of Success

As I mentioned in symptom #1, the Impostor Cycle, the OAUB says, "Oh no! I need to do it again!" The fear of success is related to the pressure having to maintain the success, or live at a new level of competence, or the fear of disrupting the comfortable status quo. The result of these fears is self-sabotage. Don't excel. Don't take a risk. Stay conventional. Don't rock the boat. Stay small. Stay quiet. Stay invisible.

Closely tied to this fear of success is a perceived "deserve level." Some people feel they don't deserve success. Life has been, and should be, hard. Earning any type of reward intensifies some weird guilt. Financial reward carries its own weird guilt, and some people feel that they don't deserve it. Perhaps it's a learned "poverty mentality" that they adopted from their childhood. I grew up in a middle-class family where my parents taught me to be almost excessively frugal. To this day, I wrestle with my attitudes about money, spending and investing. I know at some level I fear success and the financial reward it brings. What if I lose the money? What if I invest it poorly? What if the money stops coming in? Yeah, I have issues to work through.

The first step in overcoming the Impostor Syndrome is recognizing the symptoms. Now you know them. Take a closer look at these symptoms and think through when you've experienced them. What was the situation? How did you feel? What did you think? What action did you take? Feelings affect thoughts—thoughts affect actions and behavior. Now that you see these symptoms, you can stop the pattern of self-limiting behaviors.

Chapter 6

SUCCESS AND FAILURE

How a person responds to success and failure is another indication of Impostor Syndrome. Typically, the OAUB will *externalize success* and *internalize failure.* In other words, success is chalked up to external circumstances such as being in the right place at the right time, random luck, or other people's contribution. In contrast, failure is internalized as a personal flaw or deficit.

I recall an incident in PSL where I was responsible for recording temperatures using a set of three infrared (IR) imaging cameras, which are similar to night-vision or low-light cameras. At the time, this technology was cutting-edge and the equipment was outrageously expensive. I diligently cared for the cameras and made sure they were safe in the harsh engine-testing environment. However, during one test, one of the cameras sustained severe damage when hot engine exhaust leaked into the protective box which housed the camera inside the test area. It was a fluke of an accident, and no one saw it coming.

I was mortified. I was responsible for the system, and I failed miserably. How could I have made such a stupid mistake? Why didn't I pay closer attention to the signs? What could I have done to prevent this? If only I were smarter! Or more experienced. Even though we reviewed the series of events leading up to the incident and saw some warning signs, they made sense only as we looked back. Still, I felt like an idiot for missing the signs.

I completely *internalized* the failure, blaming it on my shortcomings and character flaw.

That's ridiculous. The mistake was not stupid. It wasn't even a mistake. It could have happened to anyone under similar circumstances. In fact, ten other highly intelligent people were in the control room with me, and we all missed it. The technology was so new, none of us were experienced enough to see the warning signs. There was nothing any of us could have done to prevent it. It wasn't anyone's fault, yet, in my mind, it was entirely my fault because of my flaws.

OAUBs do this. When they "make a mistake," it's a billboard announcement about their shortcomings, as well as a loud statement about their inability to evade discovery. They didn't just make a mistake. They are a mistake. It becomes their identity, and it haunts them. I can't even remember how long I dragged that oppressive feeling around with me at NASA. I was terrified to step into the control room after that. I thought everyone labeled me as "the one who destroyed the IR camera system."

To compensate, I worked even harder in PSL. Our team fixed the damaged camera, and then devised better boxes to protect all three. The next time we ran the cameras during a test, I was hyper-vigilant. Halfway through that test period, I declared, "We need to shut down the test facility now so I can inspect the cameras. I want to make sure they're okay."

The crew looked at me like I was a kook. "Maureen, you do realize how long it will take to shut down the engine and the facility, open the test cell, open up the camera boxes, close the test cell, and bring everything back on line, right?" Yes, I was aware. Shutting down the facility and the jet engine is no small task, and meant at least a two-hour hour interruption Regardless, I insisted.

Gosh, I felt nervous. I'm not sure what was more nerve-wracking. Would we find another destroyed camera, or would we find everything intact? A destroyed camera meant another failure. Intact cameras meant I was being overly cautious and even irrational. Still, I felt I had no choice, and with the lead test engineer's okay, we shut everything down.

The cameras were fine. I was both relieved and embarrassed. People told me I was right to err on the side of caution, but I still felt sheepish for causing a big disruption.

The cameras remained safe for the rest of the months of testing. The mountain of data we collected was incredibly valuable, showing trends never seen before. It was pretty cool. At the end of the project, people celebrated my work. I couldn't enjoy it. I replied with "Well, it wasn't really me. I had a great team. And we collected good data only because the cameras were protected. Anyone could have collected this data." I didn't *internalize* the success. I *externalized* it. I wasn't convinced that I was capable of producing success. Any success had to be the result of something outside of me, namely a great team and a better box.

This tendency to internalize failure and externalize success, referred to as "pessimistic-explanatory style," is linked with increased stress and depression. In 1988, noted psychologist Martin Seligman co-authored an article in the

Journal of Personality and Social Psychology titled "Pessimistic Explanatory Style Is a Risk Factor for Physical Illness: A Thirty-Five-Year Longitudinal Study." The article describes a study that explored the relation between health and the tendency to explain success or failure on either external or internal circumstances. A person with a pessimistic-explanatory style habitually attributes bad events to causes that are stable (unchangeable), global (ever-present) and internal (self-sourced). He concludes, "Although mechanisms remain to be investigated, it is clear that the person who habitually explains bad events by stable, global, and internal causes in early adulthood is at risk for poor health in middle age." That's a high price to pay. It's consistent with what Drs. Clance and Imes observed with their clients that lead them to uncover this whole impostor experience in the first place.

What if you flipped it around? What if instead of internalizing failure, you externalized it? Identify the causes of the failure that are not squarely on your shoulders. There are things out of your control that contributed to the failure. It's not all you. Don't make it that way.

Externalizing failure looks a lot like *blame shifting* so it's important to recognize the difference. Blame implies someone had a malicious intent, and must take responsibility for a failure that could or should have been avoided if they took correct action or had a pure intent. Externalizing failure seeks to identify a cause unrelated to a person's action or lack of action. It does not attribute any malicious intent. It points to things like circumstances, environment, or glitches in technology. Accidents happen. Even if your actions directly caused the failure, remember that your worth is not defined by what you do. *Failure is an event, not a person.*

The reverse is true for success. What if you *internalized it* instead of *externalizing* it? When you experience a success, focus on your contribution to it. Lay claim to your part. You did the work. You came up with the idea. You drew on your experience. Don't discount the value of your contribution. It's not prideful or boastful to own up to your talents. *When you internalize your success, you can enjoy them more. It's not entirely luck that got you where you are. You did your part.* As Thomas Jefferson said, "I'm a great believer in luck and I find the harder I work, the more I have of it."

Externalized Failure
Causes not on your shoulders
Things out of your control
Identify a cause unrelated to person's actions / or lack of action

PHASE 2

PROCEED WITH A PLAN

CHAPTER 7

STRATEGY 1: EXAMINE THE ACCUSATION

The OAUB battles an ongoing destructive internal dialog that relentlessly accuses and berates them. It's on auto-play, always chatting and sneering. Putdowns, criticisms and belief boundaries are born in the mind. The challenge becomes identifying if the accusations are grounded in truth. You must examine each accusation to see what truth supports it, where it came from and what the thought is accomplishing for you.

It's not news that your thoughts affect your feelings, and your feelings affect your actions. Your actions can become habits, and habits set the direction and tone of your life. Getting control of your thoughts is essential. Psychology offers hope. Cognitive Behavior Therapy (CBT) explains the link between thoughts and feelings, and helps people to take more constructive and positive actions by having different thoughts. it's a complex process which I won't delve into in great detail here. I will instead, propose a modified condensed three-step version that can be quite effective for the OAUB. In short time, you can arrest your OAUB fears when you *Capture* the thought, *Cross-examine* the thought, and *Counter* the thought.

CAPTURE THE THOUGHT:

In chapter 5, you learned the symptoms of the Impostor Syndrome, which means you can now recognize *in the moment* when you are in its grips. In a split second, you capture the thought as it happens. You say, "Whooops–there I go! I'm procrastinating because I'm not certain what to do!" or "I'm feeling insignificant in this conversation, so I'd better throw out a funny line so they think I'm charming and not stupid!" or "I'm not taking the time to delegate or ask for help because that makes me look weak." It takes practice to capture the thought. It takes familiarity with the symptoms, and it takes a level of self-awareness. These thought patterns have become so routine, we don't even notice it. It's like when you drive to work the same way every day, it's almost as if you're on auto-pilot, and when you get to work, you have little memory of getting there.

CROSS-EXAMINE THE THOUGHT

Next, you put the thought on the witness stand and grill it with intense focus to separate fact from fiction, and fact from feeling. For example:
- Is this thought *really* true?
- What data supports it?
- Where did it come from?
- Is it true you're procrastinating because you don't know what to do? Perhaps you know what to do, but there are many ways to do it, or different ways to start it.

- Are you just confused? Do you need more time, more information, or more resources?
- Is it really terrible to remain silent in a conversation?
- Do people actually think you are stupid if you're silent? Probably not. They probably don't even notice.
- Is it true that nobody can do the as job well as you? Is it possible there is another way to do the job? Maybe you just don't have time to explain it to someone.
- If you ask for help, will you *really* look stupid? So what if you did?
- What's the worst that could happen? Can you live with that?
- Is the stability of the free world in the balance? I highly doubt it.

Sometimes you need to dig deeper to know where the accusations came from in order to separate fact from fiction. At NASA, there was an unwritten rule for attendees at meetings in the large conference room in the main administration building which housed the offices of the top brass of NASA: only managers could sit at the table. Everyone else was expected to sit in a chair along the wall. I thought that was dumb. I didn't want to sit against the wall. I like tables better. I walked into one meeting and took a seat at the table. Oh my, based on the looks I saw on people's faces, you would have thought the world came off its axis. Well, it didn't. Did I feel uncomfortable? You bet I did–for about a minute. Then we all got past it. I didn't realize it at the time, but I cross-examined the "rule" and decided it wasn't a real rule.

As you cross-examine the thoughts that claim you are under-skilled or inadequate, you may find there's a measure of truth and you really are under-skilled. There are legitimate reasons for a person to be under qualified or not well suited for a specific job. It's okay to accept that truth without assigning any moral value to it. It is simply fact; neither right nor wrong.

In high school, I worked as a waitress in a family-owned restaurant. The owner wanted to add home-baked pies to his menu so he asked me if I could bake. Wanting to please him, I said, "Sure, I think I can do that." I immediately regretted it. I don't like to cook, and I don't like apple pie. I had never made one in my life. He said "Make one and I'll sample it." Oh boy, now I was in deep. I dug out a recipe and made a sample pie. He thought it was okay, and immediately assigned me to pie duty. Each morning, I had to make a dozen pies. It was not fun, but I kept making those pies. My enthusiasm faded, and soon I was miserable. Eventually, so were the pies. He finally said, "I think you're in the wrong job. I'll find someone else to make the pies." I was so relieved, and I was in complete agreement. No judgment, no shame.

Experience comes with time. The commitment to develop experience must come with a level of excitement, interest and optimism. At NASA, we called the recent college graduates "Fresh-Outs." They all had the same wide-eye wonder, and were spilling with promise. Most harbored that same terror I faced on my first day: "Can I do this job?" A few years ago at an IT conference, I met a female Fresh Out from Microsoft. She asked, "What can you say to someone like me who shows up for work each day and doesn't feel qualified for the position?" I said, "First of all, the fact that you earned a degree, were hired by Microsoft, and are a female in a male-dominate world–those are all great things. Own it. Second, accept the fact that because you are fresh out of college, there are many things that you don't know because you haven't accumulated the experience yet. Don't be ashamed of that. Be patient." She was instantly relieved.

There could very well be a legitimate reason for you to feel like you don't know what you're doing. It could be a true skill deficit, or a hole in your education, or you simply don't like the job you're in. That's okay. Go back to the dot analogy. You can't know everything. You also can't love every job. Vocational inauthenticity, or trying to like a job that you don't think is the best fit for you can make you to feel like you have to fake it. "Fake it till you make it" may work for generating enthusiasm or baking pies, but it's not good when you're developing software or doing brain surgery. Do what you love, and you'll love what you do. Patiently wait as you accumulate the experience.

COUNTER THE THOUGHT

This means to take decisive action. A common mistake people make is waiting to be *motivated* before taking action, saying, "I'm just not *motivated!*" The problem is that motivation rarely precedes action. Action always precedes, and then creates, motivation. This is why OAUBs don't respond to motivational speeches. Statements like "Believe in yourself! Believe in your dreams! If you can dream it, you can do it!" do not inspire the OAUB. Why? Because if it truly were as easy as believing, they'd be doing it. Belief comes hard to them. Hearing that someone believes in them doesn't encourage them because they're saying to themselves, "You believe in me? Wow, guess I've fooled you. I'm a better at faking than I thought, and that makes me feel guilty. So, on top of inadequacy, now I have to deal with guilt. Good grief." It actually intensifies his or her own impostor feelings. It's a viscous cycle.

The only thing that will work is action. After you've captured and cross-examined the thought, the next step is to counter the thought with decisive action. Action alone completes the three-step process to defeat self-doubt. Don't be pitiful; be powerful.

A CASE STUDY

Here's an example of this three-step process. I'm a member of the National Speakers Association (NSA), which is non-profit association for professional speakers. In our Ohio chapter, I met Jack Park, a well-known expert on the history of the Ohio State University (OSU) football program. Jack is a radio personality, newspaper columnist, and successful speaker. I'm a big college football fan, although my allegiances belong to my own alma mater, University of Notre Dame. I love to listen to Jack tell football stories because he's a master storyteller. One day I said, "Jack, you should write a book with these stories!" He said, "Actually, I've written a few already. My last one came out ten years ago. Maybe it's time for another."

A few weeks later, he called me, all jazzed up and excited. "Maureen! I just read a magazine article you wrote. It's excellent! You're a great writer. I have an idea. I've wanted to write another OSU book. What if we co-authored it?"

To say I was shocked is an understatement of epic proportion.

If Jack has asked me this ten years ago, I would have instantly said, "No. I don't think that's a good idea." End of discussion, but now I knew the Impostor Symptoms, and I recognized when the manifested themselves in my life, and I knew a process to work through it.

I captured the thoughts. The impostor in me screamed silently, "Jack, are you crazy? I didn't go to Ohio State! I went to Notre Dame! I don't know Ohio State football! I don't know enough about football in general! There's no way I could write such a book! People would read right thought me and figure out I'm not an expert. I'm not a good writer! That magazine article was terrible. You probably only want me as a partner because I'm charming and funny. Now you want me to be smart?"

Yes–in the moment I was fully aware of the roar of all my self-doubts. They also came with all their relatives: self-defeat, fear, insecurity, cowardice, and apprehension. It was a full frontal attack.

Then I cross-examined the thoughts. "HOLD ON! Jack is not crazy. He's actually brilliant, well respected and very successful. Why would I doubt that he sees potential in me? It's his reputation on the line, so why would he risk that just to give me a break? That can't be his motive. Yes, it's true that I am not an Ohio State football expert, but I don't need to be. Jack already is an expert. It is also true that I'm a good writer. I've written other books, and I write regularly for an international magazine, and people frequently tell me I'm a good writer. I could do this project. It actually sounds like it would be fun. I do love football. It's a little scary, but it would be cool to work with Jack. I'm willing to put in the time. It will also be profitable and exciting. And what's the worst that could happen? It's only a book about football." Under cross-examination, there was nothing I could find that would destroy me or the free world. It all seemed positive.

Then I countered the thought with decisive action. "Yes, lets do it!" I said with conviction and determination. I had no idea what the future would hold, but I was willing to take a leap into the unknown to find out.

What an adventure it was. It took two years of planning, researching, interviewing, writing and re-writing. Finally, in December 2017, we proudly released *Buckeye Reflections: Legendary Moments From Ohio State Football*. During the journey, I interviewed some college football greats like former OSU head coach Jim Tressel and the only two-time Heisman Trophy winner, Archie Griffin. My operating envelope got bigger because those experiences were not in my old one.

Dr. Phil McGraw calls it "putting verbs in the sentence." Action alone will work. Speak up. Raise your hand. Volunteer. Run for office. Enter the contest. Make the phone call. Write the check. Sign the agreement. Apply for the job. Take on the project. Whatever the action is that will push your envelope, take it. Counter the thoughts that would hold you back.

Chapter 8

STRATEGY 2: CULTIVATE SOME CONVERSATION

If the accusation is your internal dialog, the conversation is your external dialog, the words you speak out loud. Don't underestimate the impact of your words. Sigmund Freud wrote, "Words have a magical power. They can either bring the greatest happiness or the deepest despair." What do you say to others? How do you engage with your world?

There's a great paradox of the Impostor Syndrome. It's both amplified—and diminished—in community.

Huh?

Let me explain. When you are alone, you are a rock star. You feel confident, competent, and well suited for where you are. It's easy to be the star of the show when you're by yourself. When it's just you and the computer, you and the remote, you and the cup of coffee, it's easy to be great. You can think, "I'm darn good. I'm smart. I'm strong. I'm making things happen." There's nobody to judge you, criticize you or compare you to anyone else. You rock.

Then you get in community, surrounded by your professional peers, or people who you think are further along than you are, and the impostor voice pipes up. "I'm not as smart as they are. And certainly not as smart as they think I am. Am I meeting their standards? What *are* the standards? How did I even get here? I don't belong here!" Blah blah blah–the condemnation and accusation blabbers on and on. The volume of your impostor voice is the loudest when you're around other people because of the "compare-and-despair" demon. So, it's *amplified in community*.

That's the bad news. Here's the good news, and I've seen it over and over again. For example, when I speak on this topic at a conference, people walk into my session, maybe a bit nervous or intimidated. The topic description was printed in the conference program, so they all know what they're coming for. They look around and see the room filled with other people who are there for the same reason, and they instantly think, "Wow! I'm not alone. There are others like me." It's almost as if there's a collective sigh of relief from everyone, and a weight is lifted. Then they start to acknowledge their fears, and even speak about it with others. The fear is instantly diffused, and the power of the impostor experience is instantly *diminished in community*.

Don't miss this point. It's pivotal.

Cultivating the conversation means using your words and making connections to diffuse the self-doubt. When you acknowledge the value of community and the effect that verbalizing impostor concerns has on the process of defeating self-doubt, you'll be amazed what happens. Verbalize your doubts. I don't mean that you walk around with your head hanging down, feet shuffling along, flogging yourself with

"I'm a fake, I'm a fraud, I don't know what I'm doing." No, not even close. I am saying it's important, critical in fact, to realize that you are not alone, and there's tremendous value in engaging in dialog about it. If you look to the left and right of you, you'll find others who feel the same as you do. That's liberating and freeing.

Verbalizing it takes courage, but when it's well placed, it's magical. For example, if an OAUB is in a meeting and she doesn't know what's going on, she may be too afraid to admit she doesn't know what's going on. A better response is to say, "Excuse me, can you explain that one more time? I want to make sure I get it." Or "I'm not familiar with that. Let me do some more research." Or even "I don't know. Let me find someone who does." She simply admits that she doesn't have all the answers. If she's a leader, her team will have greater respect for her. It will create an opportunity for more people to be involved in the problem, which could lead to a better solution. It also reflects her strong character and high level of integrity. Most significantly, her willingness to admit she doesn't have all the answers gives others permission to do the same. Transparency is contagious.

TEACH WHAT YOU KNOW

"They all expect me to be the expert. I'm not!"

This is the script inside the head of the OAUB. Can you relate? Do you feel pressure to be the expert?

Relax. You don't need to be the expert. Nobody expects that of you. Seriously, they don't. Surely, however, you do know something different that those around you don't know. What if you taught it to them? Believe it or not, *the simplest, fastest, and most enjoyable way to overcome the Impostor Syndrome is to teach something you know to someone else.*

It's super simple. And the reason it works is threefold. First, you engage in the act of giving, which always feels good. Second, you confirm to yourself that in fact you do know something well, and that's a nice boost to your self-esteem.

The third reason is not as obvious, but still pretty significant. Even if you explain something you know to someone who already knows it, you are giving that person a gift because he feels smart for already knowing it. And who doesn't like to feel smart?

An example: a few months ago, I was the keynote speaker at an information systems association state conference. I imagined I had two strikes against me. I'm not an information systems person, and I don't live in the state where this conference was being held. I could have walked into the conference feeling odd, tempted to listen to my inner voice snarling, "Maureen, you have nothing to offer them. You don't belong here, and they're about to figure that out." Instead, I reminded myself of some of the principles of overcoming Impostor Syndrome, especially the one about "teach people something you know."

I gathered up all my courage and confidence and walked into that conference ready to teach what I know. I knew I was prepared. I had spent a substantial amount of time reviewing my material and practicing the talk. Most importantly, I believe in the topic.

The title of my keynote was *"Leadership is NOT Rocket Science."* My core message was that leadership is just another word for influence, and we all have more influence than we realize. My content was not complicated or innovative. I spoke about servant leadership, a time-honored and simple philosophy that emphasizes leading via serving, not leading via controlling. I framed it with funny stories, statistics, research, and lots of energy.

This was not rocket science. I even said, "You all know this. I'm not telling you anything you don't already know."

That's when it hit me. I didn't teach them anything new. I simply reminded them of something they may have forgotten by framing it in a new way. Their body language told me they liked it. They nodded, sat up straighter, and had that "thinking" look in their eyes. They paid more attention, and even laughed at my jokes.

Suddenly, I didn't feel like an impostor. I didn't need to be the smartest person in the room. (God knows I sure wasn't!) I showed them the *value* of what they already knew. I presented a simple concept that was packed away in the storage room of their minds, and made it relevant and useful to them. I made it about them, not me. I was on *their* cool journey as *they* recalled useful information that would make their life better.

You don't know the value of what you know until you share it with someone. Whether or not they already know it doesn't matter. If they don't know it, and you teach them, that's terrific. Now they are more informed. If they do know it, and you remind them of it, whoo-hoo!!! That's beyond terrific because now they are more energized, powerful and perhaps even committed to using the information.

Either way, your impostor can be silenced. Get out there and teach something to someone. Don't be *the* expert. Be *an* expert. Then share your expertise with others. It's your gift to give.

CHAPTER 9

STRATEGY 3: COLLECT YOUR DOCUMENTATION

This third part of the four-part solution is the most rewarding and has the greatest potential to change you. I'm also confident that you'll find it so fun it will become the easiest of the four parts to implement regularly.

By 1997, I had been the PSL Facility Manager for about seven years, and it was time for me to move on. However, I was quite concerned about leaving the job in the hands of a successor. This sounds silly, but I loved my test facility, and I wanted to make sure whoever took over my job would know enough of the ins and out of the facility to care for it like I did.

To ease the transition, I decided to write a "job manual" that detailed everything I did on a daily, weekly, monthly, and yearly basis. I described the current and upcoming projects, defined the deadlines and budget issues, and explained how to maneuver through the crazy NASA politics. I identified the key people inside and outside of NASA, including all of our customer contacts and government agency team members. I listed potential roadblocks and possible opportunities. I explained all the accounting processes, where to find the maintenance records, and even how to calculate the electric power consumption. I dumped onto paper all that I thought a new facility manager would need. When I was finished, I had 14 pages of single-spaced information. When my successor was named, I was proud to pass on this document, knowing that my facility was in good hands.

Fast-forward more than 15 years, long after I left NASA. I was cleaning out a closet at home, and I found a copy of this document. I read it through and when I got to the end I breathed a long sigh and thought, "Wow. I was good!" Seriously, I'm not saying this to brag, but I was pretty impressed that I tackled a job with so much in it. I realized that putting all my tasks on paper forced me to step back from it and be more objective about it. My perspective changed, and I could not deny the facts in that document. I rose to the challenge of a complex job and did it well.

I'm challenging you to do the same thing. Create your own job manual. Write down everything you do on a regular basis. Pretend as if you had to hand the reigns over to a successor. Write down everything he or she would need to know in order to do the job. What are the processes you use? What is your schedule? Who are your points of contact and what's your working relationship with them like? What resources to you use? What routines do you follow? What are your current projects and activities? What's coming along in the future? What great vision do you have? Put it all down in as much detail as you can. Even if you think it's mundane or trivial, document it.

Then put the document aside for a while and let it bake. Get a bit of distance from it so it's not as fresh as when you wrote it. Then revisit it, and read it as if you were reading someone else's resume or job description. Be as disconnected as you can, so you can see the complexity of the job with more objective eyes. And as you read, be aware of your emotion. Let yourself be impressed with what you do—because you are impressive.

We are so close to our own work, we can't always see the significance and impact of it. This is a quick and easy way to do it.

KUDOS, THANK YOUS AND YOU ROCKS

On the scale of 1–10 of paper hoarders, I'm probably around a 6.38. I keep way more paperwork than I should. However, the most valuable pieces I keep are the thank you notes, letters of commendation and reference letters I've received over the years. There's no better way to build up your sagging mood than to read something from someone who thinks you are awesome.

I spent years teaching a girls' junior high Sunday school class, and I lost count how many notes, gifts and trinkets the girls gave me. They've given me dozens and dozens of letters and cards that tell me I've impacted them, changed them, and challenged them. Years after they've been in my class, I continue to get Facebook messages from some of them that certainly lift me up. It's very sweet.

I've kept my NASA performance appraisals, my promotion letters, even some old pay stubs because they confirm that the work I did mattered enough to be on the payroll of the country's great space agency. I've been profiled in magazines, newspapers and NASA publications. I've kept them all. I have client thank you letters, trophies from contests and certificates from courses. I've kept them all. I keep special emails, texts and gifts from people who appreciate me. I don't keep these just to build up my ego, although that's part of it. I do it because it is concrete evidence that what I do *matters*. I don't argue with a trophy or someone's kind words. It's evidence that my dot is valuable.

Again, I challenge you to do the same thing. Collect your documentation. Find those thank you notes, letters of recommendation, awards and trophies. Read them and believe them. Enjoy them, and do it frequently. You earned them.

Resist the temptation to discount them or explain them away as luck or some other random factor. Even if "luck" played a part in it, you did your part to carry the ball across the finish line. Own it. And if the award wasn't as high as you wanted, don't discount that either. Don't confuse *being the best* with *giving your best*. Being the best is often subjective, and dependent on someone else's judgment or standard. *Giving your best* is always in your control. Similarly, don't confuse being *the* expert with being *an* expert. There's plenty of room for many experts on the same topic. And as I wrote earlier about your dot, your expertise is yours alone because it comes with your unique perspective and life experiences. Nobody can take that from you.

REFLECT ON YOUR MEMORIES

Now be completely honest. Do you have regrets? Do they darken your vision of your past? Do they fuel your fears of your future? Are you committed in your OAUB mindset to avoid any future regrets by eliminating any chance of failure?

In 2008, I took my two kids to Cedar Point theme park in Sandusky, Ohio, which is the roller coaster capital of the world. We had a fabulous time, that is, up until my purse was stolen.

Now, don't feel too bad for me. It was a pitiful lapse in judgment. I was in a hurry and foolishly left my purse in an unlocked locker while we went on a roller coaster. Oh, if I could turn back time...

Maybe you've said that. You look back on your life and felt that dagger, that sting of regret. Regret is powerful. It steals your joy and clouds your judgment. It grips you with a paralysis that makes you want to quit. Douglas MacArthur said that wrinkles age the body, but quitting ages the soul. Regret is a prison for your soul.

In 2017, the British newspaper, *The Guardian*, published an article by Emma Freud about the overwhelming (and sometimes heartbreaking) responses she got when she posted this simple question on Twitter: "What is your biggest regret?" Amidst the hundreds of replies about not being with loved ones before they died, or not choosing a different career path, one thing was most common. She writes: "... regret seems most often to be about fear. Fear of getting it wrong, leading to an unfulfilled life, followed by self-blame for being fearful."

The OAUB who is living in fear is writing the chapter of the book of regrets they'll read 10–20–30 years from now. Why fill it with fear stories?

Fear can only exist if there's been hurt in the past. Think about how you've developed some fears in the past. If you associate a certain activity with hurt or danger, you learn to predict hurt or danger when you face that situation, and you react accordingly, and sometimes automatically. The neuroscience term for making the fearful connection between a stimulus and danger is "fear-conditioning." Fear transcends all cultures and species. Interestingly, brain science tells us that of all the emotions processed in the brain, fear takes the most space and energy.

The OAUB's fears are real, and they have roots in the past. In her book, *Secret Thoughts of Successful Women: Why Capable People Suffer From the Impostor Syndrome and How to Thrive in Spite of It,*" author Valerie Young identifies seven reasons why people feel like phonies. At the top of her list is how our family of origin had a profound impact on shaping these fears that lead to self-doubts. I know mine did. I was expected to bring home all A's every report card, which I did. I remember when I got my very first C. It was in my high school sophomore English class. I was devastated. More than that, I was scared to go home because I had to face the angst of my parents who I knew would be upset. In fact, as I predicted, they were furious.

Your family helped craft your ideas about success and performance. Maybe you were considered the intelligent superstar and anything less than straight A's was not tolerated, so you became a perfectionist. Then the first time you did something less than perfect was soul shattering and humiliating. That's fear conditioning at work, making you work to avoid future humiliation. Maybe good grades earned you lavish praise, attention and reward, and you became a people-pleaser. Not doing well resulted in losing someone's affection and attention, and that was too painful. Fear conditioning again. Maybe, at the other end of the spectrum, you were raised to believe that everything you did was spectacular, that the simple act of breathing was worthy of celebration, and that you were protected from failure, disappointment, and discouragement. You were never actually taught to give it your all, because even if you gave your least, it was considered remarkable. You grew so dependent on constant validation, that when you entered the "real world" and had a boss or professor who failed to affirm your greatness, you immediately start to question your performance. That's fear conditioning—and it's unnerving.

The task then becomes rewriting your painful memories and destructive limitations so they become empowering, not disabling. If you remove the pain, you can remove the source of the fear. I'd like to tell you it's an easy "1–2–3 be set free" process, but it's not. It's a little messier than that. However, I do believe that there are two things you can do now to begin to break free from this prison of fear so you live with fewer regrets.

First, realize that your future is not completely in your control, and even if you make wise and brave choices, they may or may not turn out as you hope. Control is a mirage, and life is unpredictable. Good choices can turn out bad. Bad choices can turn out good. When you play the "I must play it safe" game, you are assuming you have control over the cosmos with the ability to guarantee a trouble-free life. The truth is our lives are a long continuum of events both good and bad, things we control and things we can't. We have to accept the good and the bad, even if we had a hand in creating the bad. Don't buy either the lie that says you can guarantee only good in your life, or the lie that says you deserve only bad.

Second, focus on what's in front of you, not behind.

In 1954, Roger Bannister became the first man in history to run a mile in under four minutes. Within two months, John Landy beat that record by 1.4 seconds. Weeks later, the two met together for a historic race. As they moved into the last lap, Landy held the lead. It looked as if he would win, but as he neared the finish he was haunted by the question, "Where is Bannister?" As he turned to look, Bannister jolted into the lead and won. Landy later told a *Time* magazine reporter, "If I hadn't looked back, I would have won!"

If you, as an OAUB, are consumed with a fear that keeps you small or hidden, won't you regret that in ten years? Won't you look back and think, "Why didn't I do such and such?" Regret is powerful, but if you look forward to the future, you can be proactive so you can live with fewer regrets. Look downstream to see what the impact of your choices *today* will be. If you have a vision to accomplish something, take a step *today* toward it. Don't freeze in fear. Look to the future, and see what could be in front of you. Make that vision crystal clear. Without that clarity, you'll lose track of where you're heading. Set bold goals. Make a vision board with an action plan. Track your progress. Make a to-do list. Join an accountability group or mastermind group. Whatever you need to do to move forward, do it. You simply cannot move forward unless you face forward. Do the next right thing by putting one foot in front of the other, and bravely facing forward. *Between yesterday's fear and tomorrow's regret is today's opportunity.* Do not miss it.

CHAPTER 10

STRATEGY 4: BUILD A STRONG FOUNDATION

The Impostor Syndrome is the result of distorted thinking. Yet, there's a strong emotional and spiritual component to it as well.

Human beings are spiritual beings, housed in a physical body, experiencing life through the senses, intellect, and heart. Most of these escape our notice because we run on autopilot. You're probably unaware of your body unless something hurts or heightens your senses. I don't notice my nose working until I smell great food or have to sneeze. You don't notice your emotions until you're stirred by something. I'm normally fairly calm, but put Notre Dame football on TV, and I'm not so quiet. Many of your thoughts are automatic and undetected, but if you have to focus on something, you bring all of your mental faculties to the forefront.

Your spirit is the same way. You may not be aware of your spiritual capacity, unless there's something that triggers a spiritual experience. It may be a tragedy, a loss, or a crisis. Maybe it's loneliness, high anxiety or deep depression. Maybe it's euphoric joy or deep love. Noted neuroscientist Dr. Daniel Amen writes in his book, *Healing the Hardware of the Soul* that brain activity research indicates that we are indeed hard-wired for transcendent experiences. He describes the temporal lobes as "the emotional brain, housing our passions, desires and sense of spirituality." He references research at the University of Pennsylvania by Andrew Newberg who studied active brain images of monks in various stages of meditation. Newberg discovered distinct changes in the specific areas of the brain that controlled a sense of euphoria and physical awareness.

Similar studies by other scientists seem to corroborate a similar change in specific brain activity when subjects thought about God. Is there really a "God-module" in our brains? Perhaps. According to British researcher David Hay, author of *Something There,* about 75 percent of the population has had some type of transcendent experience. These experiences are either a connection with a higher power, an awareness of the presence of a supernatural being, or the feeling that there is greater purpose for their own life as part of a larger plan. Not all spiritual experiences are religious experiences, but in most cases, they are long-lasting and even life-changing.

SO WHAT?

What's this got to do with the Impostor Syndrome? The Impostor Syndrome highlights *shame,* which actually feels like a spiritual experience—albeit a negative one—because it is intensely intimate and powerful. The core of the impostor experience is fear of being exposed as substandard, a feeling of shame. Many people confuse guilt with shame, but they're distinctly different. *Guilt is objective. Shame is subjective. Guilt is the result of breaking a rule. Shame is the result of not measuring up to a standard.* Guilt says, "I made a mistake." Shame says, "I am a mistake." *Guilt is rooted in a behavior. Shame is rooted in an identity. Guilt characterizes what we did, but shame characterizes what we are.*

How do you tell the difference? When you feel the sting from this accusation and judgment consider these questions:

- Did you break a rule or law? If yes, you are feeling guilt. If not, you feel shame.
- Am you comparing yourself to someone else or some standard of excellence (not a law or rule), and you fall short? If yes, that's shame. If no, it's guilt.
- Can your flaw be corrected by right action? If yes, that's guilt.
- Can your flaw be corrected by acceptance? If yes, that's shame.

The antidote for guilt is forgiveness. Usually, it's only offered after the offender pays a penalty or makes restitution Shame isn't as easily dismissed. The antidote for shame is acceptance, but it cannot be extracted from someone because it's a merciful gift of kindness or favor extended to the one who feels shame.

Noted shame researcher Brene Brown from the University of Houston Graduate College Of Social Work has spent over a decade studying vulnerability and shame. She concludes that shame is at the root of self-doubt and relational disconnect, and the way to defeat shame is to be vulnerable and verbal about your shame feelings. She proposes a "Shame Resilience Theory" that states the best way to respond to shame is to first recognize that shame exists; then identify the factors that lead to it. Next, courageously tell your story of shame, reaching out to others to receive compassion and empathy. By bravely engaging with others, being open and honest, and experiencing the acceptance you desperately want, you'll be able to feel power, freedom and connection.

Indeed, there's validity to this theory. Brown has become hugely successful and her work has been tremendously valuable in helping millions handle shame. However, I think something may be missing, which may make this approach quite risky.

This approach places the power to validate you and your worth in the hands of someone else. You are trusting that the person who's listening to you will respond with compassion, empathy, and acceptance. You trust them to preserve your dignity and affirm your worth. What if they can't do that? What if the shame you share truly disgusts or repels them? What if they don't accept you, or are faking some acceptance because they don't want to hurt your feelings? What if they're in a bad mood and just can't pull together enough empathy, or are distracted and can't focus on you? Even more significant, what if they're struggling with their own shame issue that prevents them from being comfortable with your vulnerability?

While there's tremendous value in sharing and baring your struggles with someone else, it's risky to put the weight on them to completely relieve your pressure and confirm your worth. Further, it's unfair to do that. Suppose you open up to release your burden and expect, but don't get, an appropriate empathetic response. You could feel anger and resentment, which could lead to trying to extract or demand a right response from them. That's manipulative.

I don't mean to negate the chapter where I wrote about the value of dialog with others about OAUB fears. That chapter underscores the value of community, hoping to be strengthened by like-minded people. This section warns against the dangers of demanding relief from people we think (but don't actually) possess the power to relieve. There's a huge difference between hoping for relief, and demanding it. When we hope for it and don't get it, we feel disappointed. When we demand it and don't get it, we get angry.

Another approach to responding to shame and low worth is to simply validate your worth through sheer will of self-acceptance. Assert your own worth. Treat yourself as valuable. This sounds fine, but it too is flawed. If you have no standard of worth by which to measure yourself, you'll never see exactly what your worth is, and it will become more and more skewed. It's like hanging wallpaper. Without a true vertical chalk plumb line to start, that first strip of paper could be slightly off. The next strip is off a bit more. By the time you make it around the whole room, the paper is way, way off.

In his book, *Feeling Good*, Dr. David Burns, a pioneer in the field of cognitive behavior therapy, describes four distinct paths to improved self-esteem, all centered on the topic of defining self worth. For his first path, he purports that humans have no intrinsic worth, therefore the question, "Am I worthy?" is moot. The only thing of value is satisfaction, and that's what people should pursue. His second path acknowledges that everyone has the same worth, which is neither diminished nor increased by achievement or appearance or any other external factor. Therefore, it's pointless to ask, "Am I worthy?" because the answer is unequivocally yes. His third path describes how correcting your distorted thinking about yourself establishes healthier self-esteem. And his fourth path describes how treating yourself as you would a VIP celebrity, lavishing yourself with exorbitant deference and self-love, confirms to you about your own worth and value.

These are great approaches, but what happens when they don't work?

Who can you trust to set the standard? Who can you trust to be completely reliable and safe when speaking about your shame? What is the source of both perfect standards and perfect acceptance in the face of falling short of perfect standards?

Grappling with these questions is the transcendent experience for the OAUB.

A BETTER APPROACH

I've found in my life that the source of this acceptance that most people long for is not of this world. Shame is only truly relieved with a touch from the divine. This acceptance is a gift of favor which I'll call grace, and cannot come from within oneself, or from another earthly person. Those may provide temporary relief, but true relief comes from this transcendent spiritual connection with a force, a power, a being greater than you.

I firmly believe that the most powerful weapon for an OAUB against self-doubt is to identify an external source of this acceptance. It's a sacred search, well worth the effort.

This is universal. We all long to connect and feel worthy, but at the same time, we stand behind a wall of shame. The feeling of shame is common to everyone, except perhaps psychopaths who lack the capacity to feel it. If you consider that your worth is defined from a source not only outside of you but bigger than you, you can experience even greater freedom to enjoy your contribution to the world. Perhaps the search for your worth will lead you to a transcendent experience. When shame meets grace, shame is shattered.

From where do you get your identity? Do you find it in your career? Your possessions? Your physical appearance? What happens when those are gone? What happens to your identity?

The OAUB fears being shamed because they feel they must measure up to some standard. However, if you realize that you're perfectly accepted by a being that is wholly capable of perfect acceptance, you can better survive the ripples in your confidence. Shame is shattered—but you are not.

FOR THIS I WAS BORN

Brian Houston is the senior pastor of Australia's largest church, Hillsong Church. In his book, *For This I Was Born: Aligning Your Vision to God's Cause*, he writes about meeting two businessmen, each with a great vision to build wealth, each with the drive, skills and passion to make it happen, but each with a different focus for using the wealth. The first man's goal was to "become a self-made millionaire by age 30." The second man's vision was "to fund great missionary work for his church." Both men were entrepreneurs, and planned to use their business acumen to bring their visions to life. Sadly, the first man did not succeed, as his goals were derailed and destroyed by tough times and hardships. His vision was not strong enough to sustain the pressure of these onslaughts. The second man's vision flourished, despite also facing tough times and hardship. His vision was almost crusade-like, linked to a bigger cause, giving it power and strength to endure.

Pastor Houston concludes that vision or goals by themselves do not have enough momentum or potency because there's not a compelling enough cause to fuel it. In contrast, a vision tied to a cause bigger than oneself can weather the storms and keep you moving forward. He writes, "When the purpose of your vision is not so much about you but is for the sake of something much bigger, you discover the power of the cause. This involves living a life well beyond yourself."

Helen Keller said, "The only thing worse than being blind is having sight but no vision." And something worse than that is having a vision that is purely self-focused. A truly powerful cause should be bigger than you—and beyond you.

This is so tightly linked to the spiritual aspect of overcoming the voice of the impostor. Not only will you profit from finding a source of the acceptance that shatters shame, you will do well to find a cause that is much greater than and well beyond yourself, giving something greater to aim for. Focusing on such a cause, especially a transcendent or eternal cause, can override your OAUB fears. The power of the cause will propel you past those paralyzing thoughts of fraudulence because you'll be too focused on the cause to feel the fear.

I'll make another bold statement and say this: *the most important thing that makes the cause worthy of your connection is the level to which it connects you to other people, serves other people, or benefits other people.* Building others up always trumps tearing them down. That's not rocket science. That's a lesson we learned in kindergarten.

The OAUB ongoing self-chatter of "I'm not as smart as they think I am" leaves little room for the more empowering chatter of "What can I do to boost and honor others?" or "How can I help?" When you replace the self-condemning chatter with the uplifting chatter, magic happens—that uplifting chatter can only be fueled by a bigger, bolder, other-people-focused cause.

The question then becomes, "How do I find such a cause for which I was born?"

We're back to the previous discussion about the transcendent experience and the search for acceptance. The search for this cause will follow the same path as the search for that acceptance. It's other-worldly, eternal, and available, but you need to want to find it. Get busy looking.

CHAPTER 11

SHIFTING YOUR PERSPECTIVE

As an OAUB, are you intimidated by successful and smart people? I confess that I am. Super-smart successful people, or extremely beautiful women, or influential well-known individuals often scare me a bit. In my world of professional speakers, there are the rock stars that everyone knows and admires, the ones that everyone puts on pedestals. When I meet one of them, I'm nervous. Although it doesn't happen as much as it used to, it's still there. However, I have figured out a way around it so that I'm less stressed and more able to connect with them. It started when I learned that I scare people.

People have told me that I intimidated them because I'm attractive, smart and accomplished, and that creates a barrier for them. They couldn't approach me. They were nervous around me, and they felt inadequate next to me. This blew me away. I had no idea that I seemed scary. Didn't they know that I wanted exactly what they wanted, which was to be liked? To do something that was significant and memorable? To contribute to the world in some way? To feel like I fit in somewhere? Apparently, I was preventing the very thing that

I wanted to gain. This was a huge problem! And it launched me on a path to figure out what to do about it. What I learned was a game-changer for me. I hope it is for you, too.

Let's recreate what would happen when I met someone intimidating. Let's assume it's another woman who was beautiful, smart, and successful, one that I immediately compared myself to and found myself lacking. When I met her, these were my internal thoughts. "Wow. I'm nothing compared to her. I'm not as cool, pretty, smart, influential, wealthy, elegant, strong, (fill in the blank with a mountain of other descriptors) as she is. *She won't want to be my friend.* Why would she want anything to do with me? She's so much better than I am." I'd spiral down this "woe-is-me" path.

But I wouldn't stop there. Because I didn't cross-examine these thoughts, by default I assumed she agreed with me. In other words, I'd project those thoughts as if she was thinking them about me. I unconsciously thought she was thinking, "Wow. Maureen is nothing compared to me. She's not as cool, smart, pretty, blah blah blah as I am. I don't want to be her friend. Why would I want anything to do with her? I'm so much better than she is."

Oh my gosh!

When I realized what I was doing, I was horrified. My "compare and despair" was a thinly veiled strategy that resulted in me elevating myself above her. I was subtly attributing a foul intent and lousy character to someone I didn't even know! I was actually putting her down. I painted her as a callous, even wicked individual, *which was never my intent.*

To complicate the scene, my innermost yearning was actually this: "Do you like me? Will you respect me? What can I do to earn your respect? Please like me!" I don't even give someone the chance to answer that. It's as if I answer it for them by saying things like "Of course you won't like me. I'm so insignificant and you're so awesome."

Most people have the same exact conversation going on in their own head when we meet them. They're saying, "Will you like me? I want you to like me, but I'm so afraid you won't! You probably don't like me. You think you're better than I am. You don't think I'm worth your time." If you could read their mind. (Hmmm—sounds like a song, but I digress!)

Three concurrent trains of thought are going on. One is "Please like me!" The second is "You probably don't like me." The third is "You probably think you're better than me." The first one has the potential to create profound disappointment. The second one appears to preserve at least a shred of self-dignity because it almost seems gentle and forgiving, if not a bit pathetic, and lets the other person off the hook. The third one is the most insidious one because it unfairly and illogically attributes wicked intent to someone else. It actually diminishes the other person, which subtly elevates you. This is the ugliness in this process because any time we try to elevate ourselves over someone else, it reveals ugliness in your own heart, and further diminishes us.

I'm not sure how you feel about this, but I hate that idea. It's a repulsive form of pride, the kind that keeps people away. The noted leadership expert, John Maxwell, says, "There are two kinds of pride, a good and bad. Good pride represents our dignity and self-respect. Bad pride is the deadly sin of superiority that reeks of conceit and arrogance."

The solution is two-fold. First, you shift your perspective about the other person. Then you shift your perspective about yourself.

SHIFT YOUR PERSPECTIVE ABOUT OTHERS

Shifting your perspective about other people is not hard, but it does take a bit of discipline and focused thinking. Thoughts just happen. They're automatic, and not often challenged. We just believe them, even if they lie to us. Our thoughts are based on whatever information we've gathered, and if we've gathered inaccurate information, we have inaccurate thoughts.

Thankfully, while the thoughts may not be correct, they are correctable.

Correcting your perspective about other people is based on the simple, time-tested, ages-old concept of "walk a mile in their shoes." Every person you meet is a wonderful, fascinating and vibrant package of experiences, opinions, and talents. They have a history of heartache and hurts, along with celebrations and success. They have dreams, goals, questions, concerns, fears, strengths, weaknesses, and desires. They know people they love and people that love them, and above all, they want the same thing that every other person wants: *to feel secure and significance. They want to both fit in and stand out. They want respect, love, and acceptance.* Almost all people experience a deep terror that they won't get these, so they do what they can to satisfy these longings and appear less terrified. What you see on the outside is their best effort to mask this fear. When you base your response to them on this outside package, you diminish both you and them.

One year I traveled to Las Vegas for a conference. On the shuttle bus from the airport to my hotel, the driver had to stop at about a half dozen other hotels and casinos to drop off other passengers. As we drove through the glittering shimmering casino-studded entertainment area, I was mesmerized. It's a visual delight, colorful, gigantic, and surreal.

One hotel drop-off zone was not in the glamorous and glitzy area. It was around the block, down an alley, underneath an overpass. We drove along this dingy access road to the grimy underbelly of this hotel. I could look up and see the back side of all the glitter and glamour out front, but it stood in stark contrast to where we were. Compared to the bright lights out front, this "behind-the-scenes" area was dark, decaying, and decrepit. It appeared to be inferior. However it was important and valuable. Its worth was not in its beauty, but in the function it served. The real machinations of keeping the casinos and hotels in order took place in those darker, less-spectacular areas. People are often like this; shiny bright outside, but a little darker on the inside. The darker inside is important and valuable and shouldn't diminish their value. Maybe we should take a lesson from the workings of Las Vegas. What you see is not what you get. Someone all shiny and bright on the outside has his or her share of dark painful struggles on the inside. That's where a person's value is.

Conversely, it's tempting to equate a bad appearance with a bad worth. That's just as poisonous and counter-productive. In 1986, scientists discovered the wreck of the Titanic on the ocean floor. As they pulled items from the wreck site to the surface, one thing in particular fascinated me. If you saw it you'd say "Ewww...it's twisted, contorted and distorted." But you'd also see elegant curves, symmetry and even a hint of shimmer. It was a leggy brass and crystal candelabra chandelier that once hung from the ceiling of the first-class dining room, a place of extraordinary elegance. After 80 years under water, it was mangled, and appeared worthless. When people saw it, however, they were in awe. They saw an odd marriage of damage and dignity that told a story of a silent struggle which now raised its value to a new level. People looked past the flaws and saw straight to the worth.

I recall being in the emergency room when I was in college. I had miserable back pain that had kept me in bed for four days straight. I hadn't changed or showered and was gross and quite stinky. Surely you know that when you look your worst, you have the best chance of running into people you know. So, what was the chance I'd run into my high school prom date at the hospital? Apparently 100 percent. He was the X-ray technician. I was so embarrassed because I looked like garbage and smelled like it too. I was so surprised when he treated me with such kindness, and was so excited to see me again. He could tell I was in pain, and he did what he could to calm me down, and even make me feel special...like a twisted chandelier that now had new value. I thought, "I want to do that for other people—make them feel special; look past their flaws and straight to their worth."

When I started to see people through these filters, it changed me. I started to look past the outside to see the deeper value. If there was shiny package outside, I would remember that they probably have fears, concerns and hurts just like I do, and simply want to be liked and valued. If they had an appearance that was less polished or sophisticated, I try to see past their flaws and straight to their worth. I discovered true treasures in them. I made a better connection. I enjoyed them more. The joy you can experience when you lift someone up is unmatched. And when you are busy building someone else up, you can't give a moment's worth of time to engage in the "compare-and-despair" drama. While you are silencing the voice of shame in someone else's head, the voice of shame you end up silencing is yours. That's awesome.

SHIFT YOUR PERSPECTIVE ABOUT YOURSELF

"Comparison is the thief of joy."

Either Teddy Roosevelt or author Dwight Edwards said this, and I can't trace exactly who did. Regardless, the words ring true. As an OAUB, you know this trap. Despite your impressive credentials and exemplary accomplishments, you continue to compare yourself to your professional peers. "They are smarter than I am. More experienced. More educated. More influential. They know the recent developments and trends. I'm such a hack compared to them. I'm worthless." In a heartbeat, you spiral down a rabbit hole of frantic fear and "compare and despair."

Stop It.

Easier said than done, right? It's hard to resist the temptation to scan the landscape and size up everyone. As you're trying to not only figure out where you fit in, you seem powerless to avoid condemning yourself to the lowest spot in the food chain—which is what most OAUBs will compulsively, but illogically, do. Thankfully, there's a way out of the drama.

Here's how: Ignore your *place* and embrace your *space*.

Huh?

In his book, *The War of Art*, author Steven Pressfield describes the difference between *hierarchy* and *territory* orientation. *Hierarchy orientation* is our tendency to compare ourselves against others, determining a pecking order. It's a natural default since most of our society operates on some type of chain-of-command structure. From childhood through adulthood, we stand in line according to some criteria such as height, last name, or order of appearance. As adults, we also do it with our skills and abilities, falsely assuming that we are pigeonholed according to some measure of adequacy and efficacy. By default, we assign ourselves a place in line, in a hierarchy of increasing worth and dignity as compared to other people. Our dot ranks lower than someone else's dot.

In contrast, *territory orientation* is not dependent on others; it's where you function at your best, at your peak, by yourself. It's your personal space of fulfillment, your territory of excellence, and your domain of joy. It brings you sustenance, deep satisfaction, and a sense of purpose.

Every person, including you, has some territory of excellence, a space of distinction—your dot. And because it's solely yours, nobody else's is exactly the same. Your space is your space, and only you can occupy and control it. You dance in your own theater and perform on your own stage. You excel in some aspect of art, business, humor, stamp collecting, gaming, science, cooking, writing, fitness, or politics. You are great at *something*.

Grasping the difference between hierarchy and territory is the trick to avoiding the "compare-and-despair" trap. It's simple but not easy. You must choose to ignore your place and embrace your space.

For example, I recently participated in a webinar about livening up PowerPoint slides. Prior to the webinar, people were invited to submit some slides so they could be critiqued/evaluated during the live broadcast. I submitted my slides from a recent talk I gave. When it was my turn for evaluation, the expert very kindly told me that my slides were awful. Well, he didn't come right out and say it like that. He did say they were not professional. My OAUB translated it as "They're awful! What was I thinking? I stink at this!"

Then I used my Capture/Cross-Examine/Counter approach. The fact is I did the slides myself because I was too proud and cheap to ask for or pay for help. It showed. I am not a PowerPoint expert. After he pointed out the flaws, I agreed–they weren't very good slides. He offered brilliant suggestions to improve them, and I welcomed his advice. I didn't feel like a failure or let his opinion define me or undo me because I do know my strengths. I'm no PowerPoint ninja, but I'm a darn good speaker. A stage, a microphone and an audience: that's my happy place or better yet, my happy *space*. Knowing this makes it much easier to accept that PowerPoint is not my space. I wasn't intimidated by the expert; instead, I admired him and accepted his help. I edited my slides.

If you can fully embrace your space, that is, fully acknowledge your greatness and skill in *your specific circle of fulfillment,* you will be less likely to be intimidated by other people's space. You won't be tempted to find a "place in line" or a spot in the pecking order. You'll be able to appreciate others and admire their accomplishment. When you own your own greatness, you choose to bring to the world *your* unique and precious space of excellence, and not feel less significant than others.

So, ignore your place, and embrace your space. And for goodness sakes, quit comparing!

PHASE 3

PURSUE PEAK PERFORMANCE

CHAPTER 12

BREAKING THE SOUND BARRIER

I always wanted to fly in a fighter jet, but the military isn't keen on taking civilians on joy rides, so I had to let go of the dream. I did get close, sort of. One year, the Air Force Thunderbirds were in town for the annual Cleveland Air Show, and they docked their aircraft at NASA's hangar. They hosted a meet-and-greet with the pilots and crew for the NASA employees, contractors and their families. I couldn't charm my way into getting a ride, but meeting a pilot and climbing up to the cockpit was a cool thrill.

I was dazzled by the aircraft. A supersonic fighter aircraft is an extraordinary machine with remarkable capabilities. It didn't have to move an inch to move me to awe. In the world of military aviation, supersonic aircraft are the rock stars. They command attention. They fly fast, high, and far. They go places other aircraft can't. They're equipped with systems not found on other aircraft. They have a specific mission, unmatched by that of other aircraft.

Subsonic aircraft are important too. They're the workerbees of the fleet. They are the transporters, refuelers, cargohaulers, and radar-carriers. They're heavier, slower and much larger, but can fly farther. They also outnumber supersonic aircraft by about 2:1.

Indulge me as I reach for another aerospace analogy: Imagine yourself as an aircraft. Are you supersonic?

I don't mean, "Are you living at high speed?" Goodness no! Life is hurtling fast-enough. A supersonic life, like supersonic flight, is not about speed. It's about power, influence, uniqueness, mission, and preparedness. Consider these questions:

- Are you living to your capacity, or performing short of your abilities?
- Are you using your personal power?
- Are you aware of your uniqueness?
- Do you understand you have more influence than you think?
- Are you clear on your mission and purpose?
- Are you daring enough to take on new challenges?
- Do you want to be more courageous?
- Do you feel guilty that maybe you haven't given your all to an assignment?
- Do you shrink back in the face of a challenge or shudder at taking a risk?

If you answer yes to these questions, you could very well be a "supersonic person with a subsonic mentality." Many OAUBs have this limiting mentality, as we've discussed several times in this book.

These are important questions. You may not have the answers yet, but there's significance in asking them. Believe it or not, if you struggle with the Impostor Syndrome, you are a mover and shaker, and you have potential to greatly influence the world. It shows you want to give your best efforts to get the best result. Mediocrity is not your thing. You aim high and give it your all. That's admirable. Your challenge may be to find your design point.

DESIGN POINT

At PSL, every time we fired up the engine for a test, we'd set test conditions and engine throttle level at its "design point" which represents the operating condition where the engine will spend the most time in actual flight. Fighter aircraft and other supersonic aircraft will have two design points, one subsonic (below the speed of sound) and one supersonic (above the speed of sound.) Every day, we'd record data at these design points so we'd have a running record of performance history. If we saw a deviation in performance at the design point, we knew there was a problem we needed to investigate.

For the bulk of any given test program, we would operate the engine "off-design." Maybe it was a different altitude setting, or different engine throttle setting. The goal was to examine the effect of new hardware on the engine performance. Of special significance was what the engine did in "transient condition," which was when the test or engine condition was changing, such as during altitude increase or throttle shift.

Operating at the design point was usually predictable and safe. Operating in transient, with experimental hardware, was sometimes tense. We had no guarantee about what would happen, and there was a risk things could go south pretty quickly.

What's your design point? Where do you spend the most time in your professional life? Where are you most comfortable? Where is it safe and predictable? If you stay there, that's fine, but to push your envelope, you need to courageously put yourself in a transient condition. Change is necessary.

TRANSITION IS TOUGH

"The morning of Tuesday, October 14, 1947, dawned bright and beautiful over the Muroc Dry Lake, a large expanse of flat, hard lake bed in the Mojave Desert in California. Beginning at 6:00 a.m., teams of engineers and technicians at the Muroc Army Air Field readied a small rocket-powered airplane for flight. Painted orange, and resembling a 50-caliber machine gun bullet mated to a pair of straight, stubby wings, they carefully installed the Bell X-1 research vehicle in the bomb bay of a four-engine B-29 bomber of World War II vintage.

At 10:00 a.m., the B-29 with its soon-to-be historic cargo took off and climbed to an altitude of 20,000 feet. As it passed through 5,000 feet, Captain Charles E. (Chuck) Yeager, a veteran P-51 pilot from the European theater during World War II, struggled into the cockpit of the X-1. This morning Yeager was in pain from two broken ribs incurred during a horseback riding accident the previous weekend. However, not wishing to disrupt the events of the day, Yeager informed no one at Muroc about his condition, except his close friend Captain Jack Ridley, who helped him to squeeze into the X-1 cockpit.

At 10:26 a.m., at a speed of 250 miles per hour, the brightly painted X-1 dropped free from the bomb bay of the B-29. Yeager fired his Reaction Motors XLR-11 rocket engine and, powered by 6,000 pounds of thrust, the sleek airplane accelerated and climbed rapidly. Trailing an exhaust jet of shock diamonds from the four convergent-divergent rocket nozzles of the engine, the X-1 soon approached Mach 0.85, the speed beyond which there existed no wind tunnel data on the problems of transonic flight in 1947.

Entering this unknown regime, Yeager momentarily shut down two of the four rocket chambers, and carefully tested the controls of the X-1 as the Mach meter in the cockpit registered 0.95 and increased still. Small invisible shockwaves danced back and forth over the top surface of the wings. At an altitude of 40,000 feet, the X-1 finally started to level off, and Yeager fired one of the two shutdown rocket chambers. The Mach meter moved smoothly through 0.98, 0.99, to 1.02. Here, the meter hesitated then jumped to 1.06. A stronger bow shockwave now formed in the air ahead of the needlelike nose of the X-1 as Yeager reached a velocity of 700 miles per hour, Mach 1.06, at 43,000 feet. The flight was smooth; there was no violent buffeting of the airplane and no loss of control as feared by some engineers.

At this moment, Chuck Yeager became the first pilot to fly faster than the speed of sound, and the small but beautiful Bell X-1, became the first successful supersonic airplane in the history of flight." [2]

That day in 1947 changed the world of aviation forever. The breaking of the sound barrier was the culmination of more than 250 years of exhaustive and sometimes puzzling research in the field of high-speed flight dynamics. At the time of the Bell X-1, subsonic flight was the norm, and high-speed flight was unknown. In fact, most researchers believed that supersonic flight was either impossible, or extremely dangerous. Contemporary aircraft were brutalized at high speeds. Rough turbulence made the aircraft so unmanageable and unstable that pilots struggled to keep control. Scientists feared that if an aircraft exceeded the speed of sound, the

---

[2] Excerpt from *Research in Supersonic Flight and the Breaking of the Sound Barrier* by John D. Anderson, Jr. (essay included in the book "From Engineering Science to Big Science: the NACA and NASA Collier Trophy Research Project Winners; edited by Pamela E. Mack, published by NASA, 1997. Used with permission from NASA.

resulting aerodynamic effects would violently buffet and destroy the aircraft and probably kill the pilot.

Their fears were unfounded. Supersonic flight was not only possible, but safe. The rest is history.

The OAUB faces many situations that feel a little like being on the "never-done-before" side of supersonic flight. The fear of being ripped apart by failure or discovery is paralyzing. What would happen *if you* pushed through *your* boundary? What kind of buffeting would you experience? If you are a supersonic person who's tired of living a subsonic life, choose to push past your self-imposed barrier. It could lead you to a much larger operating envelope with great possibilities.

Transitions can be hard, no doubt. When you take a risk and step into an unfamiliar world, you can expect your impostor fears will increase in volume. Don't let them stop you from pushing through to the unknown because it may be a smoother ride than you think, and with greater payoff than you can imagine.

Bell Aircraft Corporation X-1, with shock pattern in exhaust plume. Used with permission from NASA

CHAPTER 13

THE FAVOR IN FAILURE

As trite as it sounds, failure really is the route to success. I once saw a YouTube video of a woman speaking on the topic of Impostor Syndrome, where she described her own struggle with feeling like a fraud, despite being an educated and successful computer programmer. Her fear of failure held her back, compelled her to aim low and give less than her best effort. She consistently chose to stick to projects where her strengths and skills would be sufficient enough to not allow her to fail. The result was her inner voice saying, *"You are lazy. You are stupid. You are not valued here."*

Then, inspired by a new commitment to cultivate a richer inner life, she decided to try something different. This is quite fascinating since it's consistent with my earlier chapter that linked Impostor Syndrome with spiritual issues that people wrestle with. She asked herself, "What would happen if I gave 100 percent of my best effort to a tough project?" That's a powerful question–one that can put you at the precipice of great transformation.

She chose to take on a difficult project, a new product development—one she didn't think she could do because it was complex, challenging, and loaded with company political issues. She committed to going all out, doing her best to make the project a success. There were long hours, fiery meetings, and difficult technical problems to solve. She led her team well, and the product launch date drew near.

However, at the last minute, because of some unsolved technical problems, she cancelled the product rollout. In the eyes of the world, she failed.

Or did she?

She said, "It was deeply humiliating, and not without severe political consequences. However, while it was externally humiliating, internally, I was incredibly proud of what I had done." For her, the process of leading the team was rich and rewarding. *The power of the defeat was completely diffused by the awareness of her influence and untapped strengths.* She felt awesome. Further, the "failure" created new opportunities to solve the problems of the product, which cultivated a newfound spirit of cooperation and creativity in her team. Oh, and she was promoted. Pretty sweet.

Failure can be both humiliating *and* empowering—but the empowering voice can be stronger. If you are an OAUB, you may fear failure because you think it will undo you. However, failure can lead to success, albeit a success that looks quite different from what you expected. In fact, in some cases, *the only path to success is through failure.* If you ask yourself, "What would happen if I gave it my all?" and chose to walk bravely into a scary situation, you will be strangely energized. Perhaps terror may be your constant companion, and failure will lead to feeling humiliated, but you will survive. And as trite as it sounds, you will thrive. You will see that your authentic self does have value to offer. You can enjoy the failure because the personal satisfaction makes it worth it. You will see that while impostors don't allow themselves to fail, authentic people do, and the process of falling down is necessary to rise up. It will strengthen you and enable you to enjoy a newfound feeling of pride in your accomplishments.

What would happen if *you* stopped playing small, and truly gave it your all? What is scary to you right now?

For me, it was writing this book. There's a lot of psychology and neuroscience in this topic, and that's not my area of expertise. I have wanted to write a book on this topic for over four years. Every time I speak to a group on this topic, people ask, "Do you have a book on this?" I hated saying, "No, not yet." So, three years ago I started an outline. Then life got complicated, and I put the project aside. People kept asking, "Do you have a book on this?" I got tired of saying, "I'm working on it!"

The truth is I was, and still am, afraid it will be a massive flop. I've read so much about the topic, and most of what I read is so well researched, so well organized and so clearly written, that I thought, "I can't measure up! I'm not qualified."

After cross-examining that thought, I determined that there are people who I can help with my perspective, my strategies, and my encouragement. I couldn't hide behind this "I'm not qualified" mask any more. I chose to write the book.

And write I did. I approached it with full-blown Impostor Cycle in peak season. I procrastinated for a long, long time. Then I suddenly saw a deadline. I am scheduled as the keynote speaker at a conference, and I promised them I'd bring my book. Game on. I must deliver. I jumped into overwork and under-sleep mode. Seriously, I spent four straight days, from sunup to sundown, locked in my office, chained to my computer, pounding out a book. Finding content wasn't the problem. I've been thinking and researching and blogging and talking about this topic for years. I didn't lack content. I lacked discipline to organize it and then condense it. I'm wordy. Fighting through my own self-sabotage was a struggle, and I'm glad I did it. Now I worry whether anyone will read past the first few pages. Will they find it valuable? Will it help them? Will they demand their money back?

I don't know. I do know I couldn't let the fear of failure stop me from trying. Neither should you. I hope you don't want your money back. But if you do, I'll give it to you, and it will be ok. Going through this process has changed me, and that's a lesson I wouldn't have learned any other way. That's the favor in failure.

(But I still do hope you don't want your money back!)

Chapter 14

FUELED UP

Have you ever been so immersed in something that you lost track of time? You're so absorbed in something so rewarding that you feel energized and satisfied. Some call it "being in the zone," or "in my happy place." Perhaps it was a hobby, a conversation, a project that consumed your focus and energy. Psychologist Mihaly Csikszentmihalyi, renowned researcher in the field of happiness and creativity, calls this "Flow." It's defined as "the optimal state of consciousness where we feel and perform our best." Researchers have found that people who have experienced this flow state report higher levels of productivity, creativity, and happiness for up to three days after experiencing it.

One of the identifying marks of a flow experience is when a person's skill is well matched to the challenge of the activity. If it's too hard, you feel anxiety and frustration. If it's too easy, you get bored. The perfect match of skill and challenge generates a deep satisfaction. It's as if the process is the fuel source to that charges you up.

At a gas station, you have a few options to fuel up your car. Each will probably do just fine. Aircraft engines are different. Specific aircraft require specific fuel. With the wrong fuel, the engine won't work. With the right one, the engine can operate at peak performance.

Identifying your fuel source helps you to find the joy in your work, be aware of your unique capabilities operate at *your* peak performance. You own your dot. As I mentioned earlier, owning your dot will lead you to being freed from the grip of the impostor fears. You'll also understand that while you are operating under one fuel source, you don't need to feel pressured to be fueled up by something that doesn't do the trick for you.

I've identified five different fuel sources common to every person. At our core, each of us wants to Cultivate, Continue, Craft, Conquer, and Connect. They are different from personality styles identified by profile tests such as Myers Brigg or DISC. Personality is the way we enter *into* the world. The fuel sources describe what we extract *from* the world, in order to enter into the world. It's the energy we require, the fuel that lights us up. Let's take a closer look at each one.

CONNECTORS

About 15 years after I left NASA, I ran into Jeff, a former co-worker, at a wedding. Jeff, like me, served as the manager for one of the large test research facilities. Unlike me, he continued to work at NASA, and had moved on to an upper-management position.

I greeting him with a big hug and said, "Jeff! It's so good to see you! How are things going at NASA?"

"It's pretty good, actually." Jeff gave a high-level overview of what he's doing and where he fits in the agency's structure.

I asked, "So, tell me...who is still around that I would remember?" He thought for a minute; then shook his head. "I don't think there's anybody left that you would remember." He sounded a bit wistful.

I could almost read his mind. Our group of Facility Managers at NASA forged a tight bond. There were eight of us in the group, and we enjoyed each other tremendously. As we wrestled the rapids of our tough jobs, we managed to laugh a lot and support each other. We built a fortress of alliances with each other that was so strong, that even after 15 years, its absence brought on a sweet, sentimental nostalgia.

Now, lest you think this is getting too touchy-feely, it's not. The connections you forge in your work environment can be powerful and long-lasting. Our boss, John, was a master at fostering team camaraderie because of his affable personality and respectful management style. He didn't know it, but he was addressing one of the deepest capacities of human beings: the need to connect. People like to connect to other people, to a group identity, and to a greater vision or cause. Connecting leads to flourishing.

No doubt our group chemistry allowed us to get a ridiculous amount of work done, more than anyone thought possible. We were each other's cheering squad, sounding board, and feedback factory. For me, the group was a safe place for the times I felt the sting of self-doubt. I didn't even know what I was experiencing, but I know that my connections to them alleviated it.

CULTIVATORS

I live in the country, surrounded by gardens and farms. Spring is coming, and soon I'll see the gardeners and farmers doing their spring work: cultivating. They'll prepare the soil and provide nutrients for plants, with the ultimate goal of causing growth of strong trees, beautiful flowers and great fruit. They refine and develop. Cultivators in the workplace are much the same. They are the ones who "till the soil" with an eye on promoting growth. They refine their environment by adding sophistication and order. Analogous activities would be to develop or improve upon; harvest, mature, plant, tend, till, encourage, foster, promote, and refine.

Workplace cultivators are the ones to support a mission or goal. They are easy to spot because they:
- Are the administrators, planners, organizers, behind-the-scene workers
- Coach, mentor and guide people to help them realize their own potential
- Make great trainers, researchers and project monitors.
- Are list-makers that pave the way for the dream makers.
- Bring culture, order, and sophistication to the world. They decorate and beautify.
- Identify the right resources and monitor progress.
- Can make great front-line supervisors, with eyes on the grass roots in an organization.

Cultivators are significant. If you are a cultivator, embrace that, and find more opportunities to do it. Organize an event, arrange logistics, and eliminate roadblocks. Maybe you can mentor new employees or take on college interns. At NASA, I loved to get high school interns for a few weeks every so often. They were perfectly capable of doing some work that didn't require the college-level courses. My greater joy was in taking them around the NASA test facilities to show them things they'd never get to see on their own.

Maybe you can bring culture or beauty to your work area. Make your personal space more attractive or refined. In 2002, when Renny Whittenbarger, the teacher/leader of a STEM program (Project Lead the Way) at Cleveland High School in Cleveland Tennessee, allowed her female students to redesign an overly masculine meeting space, she saw a steady rise in female participation in the program, and an overall jump in the energy of the group. Cultivating has far-reaching effects.

CONTINUERS

If you've ever run into a change-resistant person who said, "I've always done it this way," or someone who laments the passing of "the good old days," you've run into a Continuer. They love consistency, predictability and stability. They want to keep the past, present, and future all tied together. They "pass the baton" from one generation to another by recording and reminiscing. They create memorials, traditions, and mementos. They take pictures, create scrapbooks, record achievements, and document events. They are your organization's historians. Jack Park, my co-author and friend I mentioned a few chapters back, is a walking, talking encyclopedia of Ohio State University football history. He speaks around the country, passing on his knowledge to the delight of OSU fans everywhere. He's a continuer, and nothing gives him more pleasure.

Continuers like policy and procedures, rules and regulations, and documentation and record keeping is their passion. They like to recognize past achievements so the future generations will value rich traditions that give substance and meaning to their work. They don't like too much change, and will often shrink back from initiating it for fear of rocking the boat. In a recent conversation with a manufacturing company who hired me to speak to their engineers about Impostor Syndrome, I had a light-bulb moment. She said, "In our company, we rely on people to speak up if they see something questionable in the manufacturing process. If they don't speak up, we have a quality problem, and that costs us money. We need people to speak up."

An OAUB with a strong leaning toward being a *continuer* may feel too timid to rock the boat or instigate any intrusion. However, if they see their voice as necessary to the bigger picture, perhaps even leaving a legacy, it could propel them to speak up.

If you are a continuer, embrace it. Without your commitment to consistency and mindful recognition, legends would be lost in time, and history would be even more apt to repeat itself. Your fuel is essential.

CONQUERORS

You probably know a competitive person. Maybe you are one. Competing is a type of conquering. Not all of us feel the urge to compete, but all of us feel compelled to conquer.

Any time you strive to win, overcome, circumvent, control or outwit, you are trying to conquer something. If you want to break a bad habit, meet a deadline, or clean out a

closet, you are conquering. Anytime you want to prevail, subdue, succeed or override, you are trying to exert your power over some conflict or tension in your world. Tension will cause a conqueror to rise up and focus on eliminating it. The tensions most often demanding relief are between:
- Man and man (relational conflict, competitions, contests, or the desire to have authority/control over another as in a boss/subordinate situation).
- Man and self (self-improvement, self-discipline, overcoming personal obstacles).
- Man and environment (disorder or clutter, organizational conflict, uncomfortable physical surroundings).
- Man and circumstances (tragedy, other people's choices, cultural issues, birth order, family background).

Conquerors solve problems, take the helm, give direction, and have a vision for the future. They are usually the forward-thinking visionaries and big-picture dreamers. Cornelius Vanderbilt had a vision for building a transportation behemoth. He started with operating ferries, then on to riverboats, then to trans-Atlantic steamships and then cross-continental railways. Conquerors make things happen, but sometimes they do steam-roll over people, and may need to reign in their powerful personality.

When an OAUB conqueror is awarded or recognized, she could still have self-doubt that poisons the achievement because she is thinking of the ways she could have done better. An OAUB conqueror may also be inwardly torn because she has a strong desire to overcome or be in charge, yet still has enough fear to keep them timid. These conquerors may instead find other outlets from which to draw their conquering fuel.

CRAFTERS

Crafters use raw materials to make something else. Don't be fooled by the word "craft." This is not about using hot-glue guns and pipe cleaners, although it could be.

Crafters build, construct, assemble, and improvise. They are the working hands that partner with the conquerors to solve problems and make visions a reality. They are creative, innovative, and independent. They like working with their hands (for example, builders, artists, designers and craftsmen) and often contribute brilliant ideas in brainstorming sessions. They may produce something physical, or they produce something logistical or organizational, such as a new way to do things, or a new organizational structure.

Crafters are both creative and innovative. Creativity, which is subjective and hard to measure, is about unleashing the potential of the mind to conceive new ideas. Innovation, on the other hand, is the application of creativity, and can be completely measurable. It means introducing change into relatively stable systems, and then determining its effect. The difference between creativity and innovation is focus. When it's focused on an organization's core goals, creativity leads to innovation that benefits the organization. If an OAUB is creative, but doesn't focus on being innovative for their employer, there's plenty of space to feel like a fraud because their contribution seems out of synch with their company's needs. This doesn't discount the value of creativity. They just need to find other avenues to express it.

CHAPTER 15

SECRET MEMBERSHIP IN A SECRET CLUB

A few years ago, I went to a retirement party for my friend Gary, a former NASA co-worker. Like Jeff, he and I were both facility managers of large research test facilities. Sharing a two-person office, we developed a wonderful friendship.

I was always impressed with Gary. He's calm and peaceful, very disciplined and orderly; he had an uncanny way of thoroughly evaluating information, dissecting facts, and making brilliant decisions. His technical knowledge was astounding. He has an extraordinary work ethic, and he got things done. He was well respected in our industry, and I considered it a privilege to be his officemate. I had him on a professional pedestal. Plus, he's a genuinely nice guy.

In contrast, I often felt completely inferior to him. I felt like I had no clue about what I was doing. Compared to him, I didn't feel smart enough. Sometimes I felt like I was in a job that was way over my head, and I was inadequate for the task. Classic OAUB!

My style was different from Gary's. I'm not calm and peaceful. I am a swirling, twirling whirlwind of energy and fizz, often leaving an enthusiastic wake of "what just blew through here?" I figured I could cover up my technical shortcomings with lots of laughter and pizzazz. I also had those constant OAUB fears of being found out as a fraud, especially by Gary, someone I admired.

The party was great. Gary and I, along with some other former co-workers, reminisced about the "good old days." We sounded pathetic, like a bunch of old people, which was exactly what we were, I suppose. Then Gary said something to the group that blew me away. I paraphrase, but he said something like, "Maureen was amazing. I never felt like I knew what I was doing, but she was amazing. She would smile and laugh, and have all the customers wrapped around her finger. They loved her. She would charm them into anything. She had such a way with people. And she knew her stuff! She knew PSL like the back of her hand."

Wow. He glowed when he said this. His smile was genuine, and his heart came through his words. I was blown away for two reasons. First, I was shocked to hear him say he didn't know what he was doing, because that's how *I* felt. Second, I was profoundly touched to hear him say he admired *me*, and my style. I had no idea. He spoke straight to my fears—straight *through* my fears. I believed him, and it felt awesome.

Here are three important lessons.
1. You're not alone in your fraud fears. If you are in the company of other high achievers, other smart people, and

other influential leaders, chances are they feel like they're not sure what they're doing either. Relax. Enjoy the secret membership in the secret club.
2. We are our own worst critic, but people around us are our greatest fans. Realize that you come across way more positively and with way more impact that you give yourself credit for. You have a stronger and more meaningful presence than you realize. You have influence, and are more powerful than you imagine.
3. While using charm and wit is a strategy OAUBs unconsciously employ to hide fear, it is a genuinely good way to be with people. Being fun and engaging is magnetic because it puts others at ease, and releases built-up tensions. It's nice to be important, but it's more important to be nice.

This can change how you interact with people. If you understand you're not alone in your fraud fears, your self-doubt will dwindle. If you truly believe that people see you in a positive way, it can change your own self-talk. It can change how you speak truth to someone else in order to silence his or her own fears If you see your own charm and wit as a great way to draw others out instead of hiding your own doubts, why wouldn't you do it more often in order to build others up?

Try walking through life believing that people genuinely respect you for who you are, that your presence is powerful and has impact. I don't mean it in a prideful, egotistic way, but in a way that releases you from fear to be invested in building up other people. As Dalai Lama says, "Be kind whenever possible. It is always possible."

PHASE 4

PERMISSION GRANTED

CHAPTER 16

PUSHING YOUR ENVELOPE

I've come a long way since that day in the driveway with my dad. My dream of being an engineer came true, and it was more fun than I expected it would be. After I closed the chapter on my NASA career, I moved on to other adventures, including running a direct sales cosmetics business, raising two kids, and becoming a professional speaker. Along the journey, I got divorced, bought a new home, launched my son off to college, and wrote that Ohio State book. Now, I'm focusing on building a stronger speaking business and doing presentation skills coaching. My operating envelope dramatically expanded. That impostor voice still creeps in every once in a while, and I need to beat it back down. When I find myself comparing my progress in my business to my peers, I come up short. I fear failing. I fear succeeding. I still have a hard time delegating. I doubt my success and influence. I am constantly examining the accusation and cultivating conversations. I collect my documentation, and I'm building on a strong foundation. My rock-solid foundation is my faith in God. Yet, a bit of self-doubt lurks in the shadows of my mind.

Self-doubt is a funny thing. Just when you think you've actually won the war, it crops up and pops up all over again.

I know. I'm right there with you.

This was the hardest chapter to write. I must have written 50 drafts, tossed around a hundred opening lines, and spent hours jotting notes on paper. I kept thinking, "What can I say that hasn't already been said? How do I end the book in an eloquent and inspiring way? I'm so awful at this!" Even when I get on a roll, and type out four or five paragraphs, I look at it and say "This is garbage. This is so dumb."

Yeah, my impostor voice, my condemning self-doubt still is alive and well. It's what Valerie Young calls in her book "Secret Thoughts of Successful Women" the dirty little secret of the Impostor Syndrome: It doesn't ever really go away, but the volume can be turned down.

I learned it from my boss.

When I was the Facility Manager of PSL, I had a performance review session with my boss John. I mentioned earlier that I thought he was the greatest boss ever. Seriously, I admired and enjoyed him. In this one particular performance review session, I told him about this undercurrent of grumbling and pessimism that was poisoning our crew in PSL. I said "John, I don't know what to do about the crew. Morale stinks. This test we're doing now is really stressful, the schedule is aggressive, the customer is demanding. The hardware is fussy, and it's always breaking down. Personality conflicts are raging, and there are wild rumors about the future of the facility. We keep hearing that headquarters wants to shut us down. Everyone's on edge."

It was a mess. I felt pressured to solve the entire problem and I didn't know what to do. I felt powerless. I told John I was "concerned." Actually, I was scared.

John calmly listened to me dump my anxiety all over his office. Then he said, "Maureen, throw a pizza party."

What? Did he just say pizza party? Didn't he just hear me?

He continued. "Maybe what they need is just to hear from you that everything's going to be okay. You can't solve all those problems. But if you let them know that you understand them, that you hear them, they'll be less stressed. Give them a status report about the current program, the headquarters stuff, and the future plans. Tell them they're doing a great job, and they matter to the agency. Pull back the curtain a bit and let them feel part of the process. Don't pretend you're in the ivory tower, making declarations from on high. Don't pretend that it's your job to fix them. It's not. Get on their level, get your hands dirty and let them know you understand. It'll cost you fifty bucks, and you'll get a big bang for those bucks!"

I was stunned. I loved the idea, but I thought, "I can do that? I can throw a pizza party? I'm allowed to throw a pizza party? Nobody's ever done that before. Is there a rule against this? Could it really be so simple? Did John just give me permission to throw a pizza party?"

I look back on that moment, and I'm amazed that I fixated on the stupid question of "Can I throw a pizza party?" Can you believe it? I was the world-known director of NASA's jet engine test facility, and I was afraid that planning a pizza party for the crew would break a rule. Talk about living within a small operating envelope.

But I loved the idea more than I feared it, and at John's suggestion, I announced the first ever "State of the Facility" address. I ordered pizza, bought pop, and even made brownies. The meeting was a huge success. I openly shared information and listened to their concerns. It was easy and fun, even when dealing with some of the tougher issue. The meeting accomplished exactly what I wanted. It cultivated a calmer feel, and a tighter team.

John's gave me permission, but not just for throwing a pizza party. It was permission for me to push my envelope. I had imagined a too-small envelope and I was hiding in it, convinced I was ineffective, or restricted by some pretend boundaries. He showed me that I have more influence than I thought, and that stepping out is better than shrinking back. It's also often easier than you expect. Without his permission, I don't even know if I would have thought about something as simple as a pizza party. I didn't think I had power to influence.

So, let me give you permission to throw a pizza party. Don't overcomplicate this. You are in control of your actions. You are the one to make the choices. But if you need permission to be great, to defeat your self-doubt in order to live with bold enthusiasm, then here it is. Don't shrink back. Step out. Your envelope is too small, and your gift to the world is too great. Get to the edge of your envelope and push it. Push it hard. And keep pushing it.

ABOUT THE AUTHOR

Maureen Zappala, a New York City native, is an award winning speaker, author and presentation skills coach. She has a BS in Mechanical Engineering from the University of Notre Dame and spent 13 years conducting jet propulsion research at the NASA Lewis Research Center (now the NASA Glenn Research Center) in Cleveland, Ohio. She became the youngest and first female manager of the Propulsion Systems Laboratory at NASA.

In 2009, she was in the top 10 out of 30,000 contestants in the Toastmasters International World Champion of Public Speaking contest. She's the founder of High Altitude Strategies, where she speaks to corporations and associations on the topic of Impostor Syndrome.

She's the author of "Great Speakers are Not Born, They're Built," "Girl, U.R.H.O.T!" and co-author (with Jack Park) of "Buckeye Reflections: Legendary Moments from Ohio State Football." She's a professional member of the National Speakers Association (NSA) and is the 2017-18 President of the NSA-Ohio chapter. Maureen lives in Medina, Ohio.

OTHER RESOURCES

Keynotes/workshops

OVER-ACHIEVER, UNDER-BELIEVER: HOW TO MATCH YOUR CONFIDENCE TO YOUR COMPETENCE

If you're a successful professional, you may be familiar with the Impostor Syndrome. It's the chronic feeling you're not as talented as people think you are, and you feel like a fake. This presentation can set you free from that haunting fear.

LEADERSHIP IS NOT ROCKET SCIENCE

Discover a unique twist on leadership that can transform a technical expert into a managerial superstar. Learn to lead with authority, passion and confidence, so your teams will begin to explode with loyalty and camaraderie.

HOW TO ADD S.P.I.C.E.[c] TO YOUR SPEECHES!

In this workshop, you will learn the "Five Non-Negotiable-Must-Have-But-Often-Omitted-Game-Changing-And-Astoundingly-Simple Ingredients" that makes every presentation an awesome experience.

Books/Educational Resources

Great Speakers are Not Born. They're Built: How to Construct Clear, Credible and Compelling Communications. Learn a simple process to put you on the path to becoming an amazing presenter...no matter what kind of presentations you make.

Power Talk: Power Techniques to Power Your Talks
In this 4 CD audio set, you'll learn presentation skills techniques to make you present like a pro, even if you're not!

Buckeye Reflections: Legendary Moments from Ohio State Football
Enjoy this unique compilation of fun facts and beautiful photographs that tell the best stories behind the Buckeye stats.
Co-authored with noted OSU sports media personality and historian, Jack Park.

Maureen is available for presentation skill coaching and as a speaker for your organization or event. Visit her website at
www.MaureenZ.com